Direct Selling- MLM- Network Marketing

COMPLIANCE SOLUTIONS

What the FTC Won't Tell You
WE WILL!

Donna Marie Serritella
"The Queen of Compliance"

Contributors
Thompson Burton Law Firm Attorneys:
Kevin D. Grimes
Kevin Thompson

Foreword:
Gerry Nehra

#1 System for Distributor Compliance
Direct Selling – MLM - Network Marketing

Compliance Solutions: What the FTC Won't Tell You - WE WILL

Disclaimer: The Publisher and the Author make no representations or warranties with respect to the accuracy or completeness of the contents of this work and specifically disclaim all warranties, including without limitation warranties of fitness for a particular purpose. The advice and strategies contained herein may not be suitable for every situation. This work is sold with the understanding that the Author or Publisher is not engaged in rendering legal, accounting, or other professional advice or services. If professional assistance is required, the services of a competent professional person should be sought. Neither the Publisher nor the Author shall be liable for damages arising here from. The fact that an organization or website is referred to in this work as a citation and/or a potential source of further information does not mean that the Author or the Publisher endorses the information the organization or website may provide or recommendations it may make. Further, readers should be aware that internet websites listed in this work may have changed or disappeared between when this work was written and when it is read.

For copyright permission requests contact:
Direct Selling Solutions
4928 Encore Paradise Ave.
Las Vegas, NV 89131
directsellingsolutions@gmail.com

ISBN: Paperback: 978-1-7350878-0-1
ISBN: eBook: 978-0-9854219-3-9
Main Categories: Nonfiction > Business & Economics > Business Law
Nonfiction > Business & Economics > Development > Business Development

The Galaxy Group Publishing
3552 Morgan Springs Avenue
North Las Vegas, Nevada 89081

Dear Karen –
Thank you for coming to the Edge program.
It was a pleasure to meet you
Best Regards,

Once you are in the crosshairs of a regulator, there is no doubt that they will join your company and the rest is a part of their basic investigation.

DONNA MARIE SERRITELLA

TABLE OF CONTENTS

ACKNOWLEDGMENTS

Jeanne (Jellybean) Fitzpatrick
For ALWAYS believing in me, encouraging me, and supporting me from the first time we met in 1991. My Guardian Angel. Thank you, Jeanne for all your love and support.

Belle Serritella
For contributing to this book and, smoothing out the rough spots! Thank you for being my big sister, you have been my spiritual connection and my example of the power of prayer in action.

Denise Michaels
For direction on standard book writing protocols. Thank you for being a friend that never quits. You inspire me to be a better businesswoman and to never take my eye off the ball.

Erin McGinnis
For asking questions, following through, and being an overall superior Compliance Department Management.

Gerry Nehra, MLM Expert Attorney
For stimulating me to pursue my business concept of providing Direct Selling Companies Compliance Department set up and maintenance. Thank you for your "matter of fact" legal advice that has saved my butt on more than one occasion. Remembering, his sound advice to me – "always side yourself with the angels."

Kevin Grimes, MLM Expert Attorney
For teaching, directing, and influencing me to do the right thing with my clients even if it meant no longer working with the client. Thank you for your exceptional legal advice and for being such a good friend over the years. We have made memories traveling all over the world to assist many clients. I am looking forward to more adventures. You have always impressed me with your professionalism, legal knowledge and integrity. Your compassionate heart and

generous giving to foster children and orphanages is a blessing in so many lives. Plus, your ability to type over 100 words per minute rocks!

Kevin Thompson, MLM Expert Attorney

For seeing my value and sharing my services with your clients so generously over the years. When some of them had no intention of playing by the rules, your expert advice gave me a heads up to watch my back. Thank you for being a bright light and a sensible voice, repeatedly, on the path to do the right thing. Your professional direction and guidance have meant a great deal to me and my business. It's been fun running through the streets of Nashville with you and Sharon celebrating repeated, successful Direct Selling Edge Conferences.

Industry Professionals

For educating me along the way through the school of hard knocks. I am honored to have had the opportunity to learn from you. Jay Coburn and the late Bob Middleton, two of the best networkers I have ever had the joy to know and learn from over the years. And, Joe Kenemore, my Mentor.

To My Clients

To all those past, present, and future clients, you've taught me so much along the way. Thank you!

FOREWORD

By Gerry Nehra

Donna has been both a business associate and a friend for over twenty years. Her professionalism shines through all that she does. Her attention to detail has always impressed me. And she constantly stays current in this fast moving and ever changing and growing industry. The compliance focus is so vital, and, I believe, under served. It can make or break a company, and I have personally witnessed more breaks than I care to discuss, and a few where both Donna & I were last minute call-ins to attempt to rescue a client but too little, too late.

This volume deserves to be read and re-read many times. She has walked the walk. I am especially drawn to the following: "Compliance documentation evidence is a priceless asset when you are faced with any regulatory investigation . . ." When a company retains Donna Marie, you will HAVE a compliance program, you will IMPLEMENT your compliance program, and you will DOCUMENT your compliance program. And that will put you on the side of the angels.

On a more personal note, about ten years ago I was suddenly called to Las Vegas for a client's arbitration, but my 14-year-old grand-daughter, Melanie, was visiting me in Michigan. Sending her home to her parents was not an option as they live in Belgium, so she came with me. And Aunt Donna stepped in to provide her travel agent like services and age-appropriate activities while grand-father did his thing. We won the arbitration, and Melanie had a memorable Las Vegas visit — Thank you again, Donna.

Gerry

PREFACE

When a crisis arrives, it's just too late!

A new world has arrived... a world in which e-commerce is accelerating and the direct selling industry is confronted with expanded opportunities for generating sales. With these new opportunities is the expanded importance of compliance. Bottom line, in the Direct Selling industry, compliance will govern the success or failure of your company. The uncontrollable consequences of many unaddressed issues can explode into irreparable damages when the FTC acquires unilateral control of your company. Having the information to preempt those events can save your business.

To prevent regulatory interference; it takes an experienced team with a proven system to monitor and track compliance efforts of the widely dispersed Distributors who must comply with corporate policies and federal regulations. Now, place this type of daunting task in the Wild, Wild West environment of Cyberspace! The fragmented and expansive Internet makes everyone trying to turn a profit online extremely vulnerable.

Many internal compliance monitoring staff personnel, while well intentioned, are poorly trained in direct selling compliance and federal and state laws and are even less knowledgeable regarding federal and state laws that address e-commerce. Such a status is a serious one. Poorly trained staff can waste time and money while potentially exposing your company to future liability. The probability for untrained personnel to overlook problems and misunderstand other company compliance issues is imminent and can be met with grave consequences. You don't want the Federal Trade Commission or any other regulatory agency to be the first to discover the problems.

Accordingly, in addition to all staff being trained to adhere to federal, state, and local compliance requirements, a Compliance Department is needed. Once your Compliance Department staff is established, effective training is essential to the success of the department. Ensuring all department personnel complete compliance training equips them with the knowledge and ability necessary to be well versed in company Policies and Procedures.

Compliance training also helps to eliminate the potential for misrepresentation by the Distributors who may not quite understand the Policies and Procedures nor e-commerce guidelines and regulations. A knowledgeable and consistent Compliance Officer is indispensable to the success of one of the most important departments in any company. A successful Compliance Department  utilizes strong staff and field leaders willing to fight for what they know is ethical and right for the long-term growth of the entire entity they are contracted to protect. This includes the company, customers, distributors, and product or service. It is short sided to expect a $15 per hour "worker bee" to possess the qualifications and/or be qualified to handle the Compliance Department is essential responsibilities. There is no replacement for the right knowledge and experience in this business.

This book introduces you to a Compliance Management System (CMS) to support all aspects of direct selling whether through e-commerce and/or other methods The CMS is flexible in application, yet rigid in design.  The flexibility allows any company to customize their Compliance Department based on its existing culture and priorities.

The rigid design allows for limited mistakes since following the system provides templates to limit those mistakes. Each company is invited to apply the Compliance Management System (CMS) based on their own specific needs and goals. The initial tasks involved in creating an effective Compliance Department are fundamental.

Therefore, it is unwise to omit any task involved in the setting up of an effective Compliance Department; since the practice of neglect can land your company in some serious "hot water." Each step included in the system is derived from experiences of actual legal discovery in the case of a regulatory investigation.

The Compliance Management System (CMS) is your company's playbook for success in avoiding compliance headaches. The CMS can help build the foundation for your Compliance Department for many years to come. Your decision to include the CMS in your company is compliance structure is a wise choice and invaluable for your success.

This system provides the foundation for our tailor-made system of compliance solutions. We have helped Direct Selling companies since 1991, we can help you too! Moreover, many additional services are available as your specific needs arise.

However, this CMS defines and describes the Standard Operating Procedures (SOPs) for a Compliance Department that is exclusive to the direct selling industry including direct sales that occur through e-commerce. The CMS is inclusive of many elements of the Compliance Department.

But, while the CMS does specify rules and policies for consideration, the manual is not the most critical piece of your compliance puzzle. The most critical component of any company is the people who make up the Compliance Department (the compliance team). It is their responsibility to plan, implement, enforce, monitor and educate people regarding the business of compliance. The CMS is a formidable tool that equips the team with the galvanized knowledge necessary to refine their skills and  foster the confidence to investigate and enforce the policies of the company.

As you are already aware, compliance issues can and will make or break a company and should not be taken lightly. Distributors can cause unwarranted exposure for a company simply by making unsubstantiated product and income claims in cyberspace.

Through e-commerce and/or other electronic means, these assertions quickly reach a huge number of people without the company being aware of the exposure. Unfortunately, most distributors don't understand the legal implications of their actions and how they expose the company by engaging in non-compliant activities. Compliance protection is one of the most sought-after and most overlooked objectives in our industry.

The CMS will provide the outline for you to set up a proper Compliance Department. Just knowing what to do is not enough. Today, many companies are in the same position. They know what they need to do, but don't do it. In order to get a leg up on compliance, you need a plan and you must act on the plan on a daily basis. If not you, then someone else must be responsible for the management of the Compliance Management System. There are several reasons to use this CMS as part of a fully organized Compliance Department.

8 Reasons to Have a Robust Compliance Department

When a crisis arrives, it's too late to prepare!

1. Protection:

Building a robust Compliance Department for your direct selling company provides protection for a tremendous number of reasons. It provides protection for your customers, your independent distributors, your company, the brand, the products, AND the general public. They always say, protect the house at all costs and make sure you have smart, effective compliance in place. This protection will help you (sleep?) better at night. Why? Because you know you must have an active Compliance department to prevent the headaches and massive problems that can happen when Compliance is ignored.

2. To Uphold Policies:

Your policies are everything when it comes to providing a solid company foundation. A legally sound set of policies and procedures professionally enforced by a Compliance Department who knows the law is critical. Until then it's virtually impossible to hold Distributors accountable to their actions out in the field. Don't just borrow a set polices  from another company. That's like borrowing a Compensation Plan. You don't truly know what you're getting. There are key sections to policies that must be customized to align with your culture and company. Be honest, will you read a 44-page document designed for another company to know what their violations and sanctions are? *Seriously?* Policies designed for your company from an MLM Expert Attorney can make a big difference.

A Master Intake Log is established to track the coordination of reported violations, sanctions and result of communication with Distributors. Correct documentation is essential for Compliance Department protocol. The result is your company has a written history of enforcement Federal Trade Commission regulators look for when evaluating compliance procedures. This is necessary because it provides an invaluable layer of protection to your long-term Compliance Action Plan.

3. Reduces Time & Stress:

Owners and corporate staff, even distributors, spend countless hours addressing compliance issues, which is not smart. In fact, it's counterproductive for the owner or founder to be responsible for Compliance Management. It is NOT the role of the owner, the owner's spouse or a distributor to take on Compliance and all it entails. Doing this weakens the relationships you've worked so hard to establish.

When an objective, neutral party runs Compliance properly and efficiently, you delegate that headache to others, and they update your staff and field leaders regularly. When owners try to perform these duties, it creates conflict in the field and is ineffective. Preparation is a must. A Compliance expert will set up your department the right way by including intake, evidence collection, monitoring, and communication with Distributors (both one on one and as a group). Education and follow up are crucial for success. It will also reduce time and stress for you, so you can focus on growing your business.

4. To Monitor the Field for Compliance:

A robust Compliance Department must include comprehensive and documented monitoring system. Your company is responsible for monitor the field for non-compliant activities.

With social media's pervasive nature in almost everyone's life, part of your Compliance Strategy MUST include Social Media Management. Just addressing closed Facebook groups and testimonials within them alone is a full-time job. Social Media is known as a place where regulators go to look for 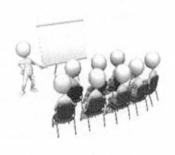 compliance violation, so don't think what goes online disappears. It does not. Evidence proves Social Media is a hot bed for non-compliant activities.

Don't keep your head in the sand. Clearly, this is a job for more than one person in a medium-size company. Large companies must have a Compliance team of skilled, experienced people. We have an experienced team who work diligently on our client's behalf to monitor manually. It works much better than digital monitoring. There are far too many cases of brand use that are missed when digital monitoring is used.

It's a mistake to not include manual monitoring in your long-term Compliance Action Plan. Manual and/or digital monitoring efforts can be more effective when utilized simultaneously. Digital monitoring is not enough. It cannot find the multitudes of violations that manual monitoring does. It takes a smart person to do this job efficiently.

5. Establishes Sanctions:

The Compliance Department is tasked with assessing the issues and implementing sanctions or consequences for the actions of their distributors. Included in your policies right now are sanctions. It would be smart to review what's been established in your Policies before a Compliance issue comes up.

Sanctions can include:
- Monitoring a distributor's conduct over a specified period of time to assure compliance.
- Issuing a written warning or requiring a distributor to take immediate corrective action.
- Imposing a fine which may happen immediately or withheld from future commission payments.
- Withholding commission payments until the Distributor provides adequate assurance of future compliance. Suspension from participation in Company events, rewards, or recognition.
- Suspension of his or her Distributorship and position for one or more pay periods.
- Involuntarily terminating the Distributor Agreement and position
- Any measure the Company deems feasible and appropriate to resolve injuries caused by the Distributor Policy violation or contractual breach
- Legal proceedings for monetary or equitable relief.

Each company can define their own policy sanctions based on their culture and what are considered reasonable consequences for their violation. Remember "sanctions" have already been established in your policies. Some companies even define what violations hold what sanctions long before any actions are necessary. It is up to the company to equally issue sanctions based on behavior. In some cases, when a more serious one is violated, it may be worthwhile to have your attorney advise the most legally advantageous sanctions for the situation.

It may be hard for an owner to hand out sanctions to their highest leaders or distributors who have become good friends over the years. This is another powerful reason to have a Compliance Department.

6. Provides a Process for Escalation:

A Compliance Department indicates the company has Compliance Standard Operating Procedures (SOP) which clearly outline the process for handling a violation from start to finish. The SOP's indicate by a flow chart the exact path of how a violation is treated. Each step is as important as the next and cannot be eliminated. The violation intake process provides for initial documentation of the issue using the 5 W's (what happened, when, to who, where and if known, why) and as much information as possible is collected regarding the issue or case.

Once a case has successful passed intake, it is vital to gather evidence supporting the case. Do NOT take the word of the reporter as gospel. An effective compliance team will research and request supporting evidence. Evidence can be an email, a messenger, a letter, a text or a phone recording. Anything that substantiates the claims is required. The last thing you want is a "he said, she said" situation.

Once a violator has been notified repeatedly and does nothing, it may be time to escalate the case to your legal team. It's prudent to escalate cases involving fraud, theft, criminal behavior, extreme poaching and more. The Compliance Department is always the entity that escalates the process resulting in enforceable consequences.

Escalation to an attorney requires a case history to provide documentation. Give your attorney all the information you've collected on the case in writing. The Compliance Officer will stay with the case. If it escalates, they stay in the loop and continue providing a written report for the attorney. Some attorneys may want the Compliance Officer to send one last letter from the company before the legal team takes it shot.

7. To Educate:

Once a Distributor clicks the "Agree" button pertaining to Company Policies, they rarely think about those policies again. In the eyes of the regulators, the company is responsible for providing compliance training to the entire field team.

Virtual compliance training is becoming increasingly popular as a necessary part of your compliance strategy. More and more companies elect to provide a customized compliance-training course for distributors. Many require the successful completion of this course to be authorized as a Distributor. The secret to compliance in the direct selling industry is continuous monthly compliance training for all distributors. Randomized testing is highly recommended.

Training can come in a variety of methods. When a new Distributor signs up, a welcome letter can include a sentence about compliance responsibilities and introduce the Compliance Course. When the new Distributor enters their website back office for the first time, a pop-up may appear stating the Compliance Course is a requirement to become a Distributor. Some companies provide a "click here video" that outlines the company's compliance policies. The basic information is taught - no URL's with the company name which violates the company trademark; no emails with the company name in it unless it is part of the self-replicated name. Some important things taught during the initial phase of compliance training includes, how to recognize and avoid making claims, disease and drug claims, and income claims. It's time saving to teach the poaching and cross-recruiting policies. These issues can pop up and result in a Distributor being terminated. It is only fair they've been educated about the perils of drug claims, income claims, poaching and cross-recruitment activities before it becomes an issue.

Training should be broken into snippets taught in bite-size pieces. It's easier to remember, and it provides an opportunity to reveal why the violation is critical to the importance of a viable organization. When Distributors understand why, the training is much more effective.

8. Prepares and Maintains Compliance Documentation:

Documentation, documentation, documentation is as important and maybe more so, than location, location, location is to Real Estate.

Documentation often wins cases. Sometimes it is difficult to get a Distributor to see their wrong ways. Even when considering evidence, some leaders deny guilt and place blame on others for their transgressions.

In the case of a regulatory investigation, preparation is key, and the department must keep accurate, easily retrievable documentation which provides evidence of an active working Compliance Department. It is negligent to have Policies and Procedures in place but do nothing to enforce them. In fact, it's almost worse than having no policies at all.

In conclusion, we've identified numerous reasons for having a "robust" Compliance Department. The company that can easily prove the existence of an active Compliance Department is in far better shape when a regulator knocks on the door. An active Compliance Department is key, so don't overlook the power and safety of having one.

Thank you for allowing me to share with you some of the reasons why a working Compliance Department is essential to your ongoing success. If you have any questions on how to effectively set up your department up, let me know. Ask about how to provide your blueprint for it in my exclusive Compliance Management System (CMS).

COMPLIANCE
MANAGEMENT
SYSTEM

Chapter 1

DIRECT SELLING IN A SOCIAL MEDIA WORLD

Introduction

SHOPPING IS and always will be a therapeutic experience for millions. Shopping reduces sadness and generates feelings of personal control. The best part is that the benefits of a shopping experience can produce long term results.

But now, the shopping landscape has changed. People in search of a little retail therapy or simply seeking much-needed necessities, don't merely jump in the car and find their consumer solutions at brick-and-mortar retailers. Instead, dressed in the most relaxed, comfy clothes, sitting in an equally comfortable chair and accompanied by their favorite electronic device, they engage in the highly satisfying act of Seeking, Finding, and Purchasing, all with a few clicks. Then, like their excited younger selves waiting for the arrival of Santa Claus on Christmas Eve, they live in high expectation until their purchases arrive.

Here's an example of products and services you can buy online:
- Cars, trucks, boats and any kind of vehicle an engineer can conjure up.
- Groceries from the store down the street or halfway around the world.
- A handyman to help with repair projects or a babysitter to watch the kids.

- An elegant meal from a restaurant for dining in - just add candles.
- Furniture, rugs, lamps and anything you can imagine for your home.
- Nutritional Supplements

This new option known as online shopping, has created a virtual world of enjoyment for both buyers and sellers who supply consumers' needs. Have you ever gone to a mall (or several) and couldn't find the right color, size or model of something you wanted? This is an incredibly rare experience when consumers shop online. Envision buying satisfaction every time, without leaving the comfort of home.

Digital Commerce 360, an industry research leader, released an article which confirms the extraordinary e-commerce business growth found in the world of online retail business. Utilizing data from the U.S. Department of Commerce, it was reported buyers spent $517.36 billion with online retailers in 2018 alone. This represented a 14.9 percent increase over the $449.8 billion dollars spent in 2017.
(Ali, F., (2019) https://www.digitalcommerce360.com/article/us-commerce-sales/)

To achieve success as e-commerce entrepreneurs, direct selling companies like any other company, must know their target market audience. Both the company and team members must be aware of how to capitalize on opportunities to satisfy a consumer's needs, wants, and desires, for goods and services via the e-commerce marketplace.

Direct Selling Organizations and Online Opportunities

Declining sales among traditional retailers co-aligns with an even greater growth in the number and size of e-commerce opportunities for multi-level marketers. Additionally, e-commerce opportunities have expanded the market for MLM companies. They can limit their reliance on domestic consumers and for perhaps the first time include global buyers. It's estimated e-commerce generated $2.3 trillion in 2017 worldwide. In 2019, this number is expected to balloon to $4.5 trillion. That's almost a doubling in two years. Direct Selling organizations are perfectly positioned to include themselves in this exploding market opportunity.

Like e-commerce businesses in general, Multi-Level Marketing (MLM) companies must be highly sophisticated and continuously refine and shift their marketing strategies. The most successful e-commerce Direct Selling companies clearly grasp marketing principles including those listed below.

Marketing Strategies for Direct Selling Companies Must:
- Understand the essential nature of well-designed, easy-to-navigate websites that retain buyer interest, including both customers and distributors.
- Develop loyal consumers by avoiding and eliminating customer service problems which lead to highly-publicized consumer dissatisfaction.
- Engage and have a robust presence in the new media called, "Social Networking".
- Recognize the world is now their marketplace and incorporate language translators and global shipping to overcome the barriers of language and distance.
- Carefully define target markets and craft both messages and products to resonate with primary and secondary audiences
- Provide 24/7 instant access and continually update digital e-commerce tools to make the buying experience more streamlined and advance sales.
- Offer fast, faster, and the fastest order fulfillment to maintain and grow a consumer base.
- Utilize marketing copy which highlights any guarantees and easy return policies.
- Identify niche markets so companies can target messages and goods to groups of consumers who are commercially

underserved.

- Access well-documented research on buying behavior of not merely demographic market segments, but psychographic profiles as well.

- Implement measures to increase the volume of each online transaction so the net return on each order increases along with the number of orders.
- Ensure their e-commerce websites are readily available across all electronic platforms.
- Avoid the "stillness" of some e-commerce sites by utilizing a live chat system to answer consumer questions in real time as they're shopping.
- Eliminate unanticipated costs which dims enthusiasm, and leads to purchase abandonment.
- Sell products on social media platforms like Instagram as well as on e-commerce sites.
- Utilize clear, descriptive and effective photos of products offered.
- Finally, remember to also provide other state-of-the-art marketing approaches.

Many e-commerce, Direct-Selling companies focus their energy exclusively on sales and marketing while paying little attention to Compliance. As a result, they threaten their overall E-commerce success story by failing to comply with regulations. This is a huge oversight.

When these e-commerce businesses are also Direct Selling companies, the need for understanding and complying with regulations becomes exceptionally important. In fact, it's almost more important than Direct Selling companies that operate exclusively offline. After all, regulators need only see a page on your website or in a social media post to start an investigation on your company.

MLM Regulations

Knowing and adhering to regulations Distributors now utilize e-commerce and social networking to expand sales. These Distributors previously sold associated products and services directly to consumers via face-to-face selling. E-commerce flipped the script and changed this formula, adding telemarketing, e-mail, voicemail, direct mail, social kiosks, text messaging, and other electronic strategies to grow their network while simultaneously  expanding sales. However, Direct Selling Companies were already heavily regulated, therefore when Distributors participate in the growing online marketplace, new areas of compliance exposure combined with Direct Selling specific regulations, creates new threats as well as new opportunities for Direct Selling companies.

Let's take a moment to review by asking, "What are the key compliance guidelines that must be followed for businesses to engage in Direct Selling?"

Key Direct Selling Regulations

The Federal Trade Commission's regulations regarding Direct Selling are generally well-known by people in the field. All persons or organizations who engage in e-commerce are participants in a form of Direct Selling. However, most e-commerce sellers have only one "tier" of distributors. As a result, they don't fall under the umbrella of a multi-level marketing business. The principles at the foundation of Direct Selling are based on a simple mathematical formula: additive growth vs. expediential growth. While most e-commerce businesses seek to advance sales along only one tier creating additive sales growth, the concept of multi-level marketing is based on the notion of increasing sales by exponentially growing the sales organization. Simply put, direct selling companies are constructed on the notion if ten salespeople grow their direct sales by ten percent per month, a certain level of revenues will be generated based on sales.

Despite the soundness of the concept, some Direct Selling companies subordinate product and services sales to organizational growth. In other words, there was a greater focus on growing a massive base of distributors rather than sales growth. This practice led to Federal Trade Commission establishing requirements as listed below.

Key Compliance Requirement #1 Income Disclosure:
Whether the direct sale occurs online, in person, and or by another means, the FTC requires that the income statement reveal that the primary revenue streams of the company are generated by the sale of goods and services to external buyers who are not organization-ally connected to the company. It's called an Income Disclosure Statement or IDS.

Key Compliance Requirement #2 Customers Required:
An audit of the financial rewards must also reveal that the compensation paid to Distributors is a result of the actual sale of goods and services to external buyers rather than fees paid for the expansion of the sales team.

Key Compliance Requirement #3 Testimonials:
Direct Selling companies, in recruiting their sales team, must not directly and/or by implication and/or images or testimonies, generate an inflated image of the earnings associated with Direct Selling participation. The testimonials and/or other marketing materials used should generate realistic images of potential earnings that have been calculated as the mean of earnings that occurred based on past participation.

Key Compliance Requirement #4 - International:
If your company sales its goods and services in different states and/or worldwide, an array of other compliance guidelines are operational.

If your Direct Selling Company sells through e-commerce, other compliance rules exist. As mentioned, because e-commerce or online sales have now become a primary venue for direct sales, regulations

to protect buyers in the e-commerce space must also be strictly observed.

Summary

Numerous combinations of compliance issues emerge anew when both direct selling and e-commerce are partnered. Other chapters in this book will demonstrate the importance of an actively functioning Compliance Department to oversee these matters. While compliance issues may seem overwhelming or onerous to the novice, highly successful direct selling businesses who have successfully navigated the crosshairs of these compliance issues do exist.

Chapter 2

WHAT IS YOUR COMPLIANCE EXPOSURE?

Protecting it ALL

ARE your company's compliance issues driving you nuts? Is everything regarding your compliance efforts falling on your desk or worse, falling through the cracks?

As a direct selling company owner/founder or CEO, you MUST protect your company. You must also protect the public, the Distributors, the customers and let's not forget the company brand. The bottom line is that it's the owner/founder's job to protect it ALL.

Your Compliance Department's ultimate responsibility is to protect the company. Remember, the Distributors are in fact an army of volunteers. They are free spirits who have joined your company for the freedom it can provide them from the 9 to 5 trap. This means a few Distributors will play fast and loose with the rules when you're not looking.

It is sometimes difficult for the executive team and the compliance team to be on the same page; therefore, the Compliance Officer is that objective person in charge of conducting investigations and managing the department's effectiveness.

Executive teams must be clear about what they expect from their compliance team. If you don't make your expectations clear, your Compliance Officer will never produce to your expectations. It is neglectful to think or expect that your Compliance Officer is to handle every aspect of your compliance needs. Executives must be sure to follow up with the Compliance Team on a regular basis best done by conducting weekly or monthly reports and/or meetings because the Executive Team must always also be aware of the Compliance Department's activities.

Brand Protection Why Be Concerned?

Do you know how important your brand is to your business? Do you know what your brand is? It is not just your logo - it is all your intellectual property. It is your domain name, your emails, your photos, your website and anything that projects the image of your company.

Your brand is your livelihood and you must protect it. This includes securing your URL's (Domain Names) and email addresses so Distributors cannot intrude and secure them. People will purchase your URL's and similar URL's then attempt to sell them to you, hence the importance of brand protection.

Claim your URL and make sure the person putting together your website doesn't own it. Many times, website designers register the domain name in their entity name, then attempt to sell it to you for a very high price or charge you an expensive hosting rate for your website once they see that your company is profitable.

Today, the Internet provides many forms of available social media, and we can only imagine what to expect in the future. If your company does not have a Social Media Plan, then get one, quickly. Without a plan, you could be missing out on a wave of the future, a brilliant marketing tool that will contribute to the growth of your company.

Wouldn't it be beneficial to know who is talking about you and your brand online, and what they are saying? Wouldn't it be even better to be able to communicate instantly with the posting party?

Direct Selling Solutions has been searching for software that would be helpful in seeking out online violations. We have found a platform that aggregates many of the online social media platform's posts. It is an incredible resource that will assist in discovering potential online violations. Yes, it is true; for a reasonable fee, you can set up your company to look at and respond to immediate posts online that may be affecting your brand.

What Are Your Compliance Exposures?

When you bring Direct Selling Solutions in to assist with your compliance efforts, the first thing we do is a needs assessment to evaluate your compliance exposures. The needs assessment, once conducted, provides vital information on your company like where your compliance necessities are and will assist in determining a roadmap for developing solutions to your compliance requirements. Once we have developed a good understanding of your needs and identified your red flags; then we will formulate a strategy to address them one by one. We will also examine your online presence; Social Media activities, your reputation in the industry, your marketing materials to include your compensation plan, flyers, charts, and much more.

When Distributors are representing themselves and your company, you hope it is in the best possible light because your company has exposure every time there is an opportunity meeting or whenever a distributor introduces your company to prospects. Believe it or not, your Distributors are one of your highest exposures, as when sharing your company and your compensation plan with prospects there could be misrepresentations by distortion or falsification of income (income claims).

Two solutions to the distributor exposure issue are compliance training and auditing of events. Compliance education is the number one way to secure your compliance efforts. It's extremely beneficial to have your compliance team audit meetings to know exactly what is going on when you are not there. Teach your Distributors compliance do's and do nots. Teach them what makes an illegal pyramid illegal. And then teach them why you are not one.

The bottom line is compliance education is truly the answer to keeping a team of 100 or a team of 100,000 in compliance. Ultimately, the company is responsible for what the Distributors do, so teach them and reward them for correct behavior. If Distributors must know what they have to do to stay compliant, otherwise your compliance team will be swamped with reports of infractions, hence the importance of training. Teach Distributors the correct behavior from the very beginning. Open their experience with your company by building credibility for your brand and showing your company's commitment to compliance.

Compliance education is an immeasurable benefit that demonstrates responsible continuity, which proves that your company is aware and actively committed to compliance; guarding against and demonstrating preparedness for a regulatory investigation - After all, isn't that the goal.

The Compliance Needs Assessment

A Compliance Needs Assessment is a great place to start. An assessment will evaluate exactly where the company should begin with its compliance efforts by examining what is currently happening in the field. This assessment helps to determine the top priority, the regulatory red flags or concerns as well as where and how to begin at getting your business up to speed with compliance.

Compliance concerns take priority, consuming the time and

dominating the efforts of the Compliance Department until actions are documented and corrected. In older companies, it's possible that some of the Distributors are dangerously increasing legal exposure for the company.

Often in start-up companies, there could be one rogue Distributor on social media and other advertising avenues creating adverse influences. Those actions could spoil it for many, so it is important bad habits be unlearned by re-training on the proper compliant techniques of advertising their business.

The Needs Assessment assists me in getting a big picture view of the company. Having an opportunity to look inside a company during the need assessment phase allows me a bird's eye view of what is happening with your compliance efforts, as well as affords me an opportunity to observe and bring awareness to other areas of concern within the company. Since compliance affects all aspects of your business, it is important to analyze each area of concern to ensure all aspects are understood and attended to, accordingly.

In my opinion, there are 16 major Compliance exposures for any direct selling company:

1. Customers or lack of them
2. Poor planning & lack of implementation of a Compliance Management System
3. Poor product value
4. The Distributors
5. The Executive Team
6. The Compensation Plan
7. Income Disclaimers
8. Income Disclosure Statements (IDS)
9. The lack of compliance training
10. Testimonials
11. Social Media & Online Reputation Management
12. Sales Literature and Marketing Materials
13. PCI Compliance and Merchant Accounts

14. Third party websites
15. Events
16. Asset Protection and Capital Preservation

"Customers are good for business."
Kevin Grimes, MLM Expert Attorney

REAL customers required!

In the world of direct selling, one of the largest exposures is the lack of customers. First, we need to define what a customer is. A customer is not a distributor but buyers of the product or service simply because they like it and want nothing more than to use the product.

Direct selling companies can have increased exposure from counting their participants who purchase the product and become Distributors simultaneously. This is called self-consumption. Counting a distributor as a customer can be problematic if you only have Distributors and no outside customers. A well-balanced company needs both Distributors and customers, independent of one another.

Case Study: VEMMA
According to the Federal Trade Commission, Vemma, was an Arizona-based Nutrition Company in business from 2004 to 2015. (https://www.ftc.gov/news-events/press-releases/2016/12/ vemma-agrees-ban-pyramid-scheme-practices-settle-ftc-charges)

Before closing their doors, they expanded throughout the U.S and several foreign countries and took in more than $200 million a year in revenue in 2013 and 2014. Under a settlement with the Federal Trade Commission, Vemma Nutrition Company ended the business practices that the FTC alleged were a pyramid scheme.

The multi-level marketing (MLM) company, which sold health and wellness drinks through a network of Affiliates called "Affiliates," was prohibited (under a federal court order) from paying their Affiliates. The only acceptable way to pay them was if a majority of that affiliate's revenue came from sales to real customers rather than other Affiliates. The order also barred Vemma from making deceptive income claims, and unsubstantiated health claims.

According to the complaint, the defendants encouraged participants to buy products to qualify for bonuses and to recruit others to do the same. The result was a pyramid scheme that compensated participants mainly for recruiting others rather than for retail sales based on legitimate customer demand for the products.

Under the stipulated order announced September 1, 2016, the Vemma companies and the owner, BK Boreyko, were banned from any business venture that:

- pays any compensation for recruiting new participants;
- ties a participant's compensation or an ability to be compensated to that participant's purchases; or
- pays a participant compensation related to sales in a pay period unless the majority of the revenue generated during that period, by the participant and others the participant has recruited, comes from sales to non-participants.

The order also bars these defendants from involvement in any pyramid, Ponzi, or chain marketing schemes, and prohibits them from making misrepresentations about the profitability of business ventures or the health benefits of products. The order imposed a $238 million judgment that was partially suspended upon payment of $470,136 and the surrender of certain real estate and business assets. It also required Vemma to provide compliance reports from an independent auditor for 20 years. [FTC.Gov]

Poor Planning & Lack of Compliance Management System Implementation

Have you ever heard the expression: Lack of planning on YOUR part, does not constitute an emergency on my part?

Develop a written plan and reduce your regulatory footprint. Use the Compliance Management System to track and document all compliance issues: track social media, monitor, educate and guide your distributor team. Owners/founders must keep a finger on the pulse of the Compliance Department without micro-managing.
When Direct Selling Solutions is on your compliance team, we develop an action plan, Compliance Department goals, and monthly compliance topics (Comprehensive Standing Operating Procedures CSOP).

Poor Product Value

Gerry Nehra taught me that direct selling companies must have products with intrinsic value. Customers must want to buy the product outside of the income opportunity. Gerry's blog post below spells out the product criteria.

Contributed by Gerry Nehra, Direct Selling MLM Expert Attorney
"Pyramids and endless chains are illegal in the U.S. You cannot "pay to play." That is why no company offering you an income opportunity with multi-level compensation can charge you anything to join or can require you to purchase products or services to join. The only exception is that a requirement to purchase at cost, non-commissionable sales or starter kit is permitted. Another way to say this is that you cannot be charged for the right to recruit others. Such a "charge" is prohibited as an illegal "headhunting fee."

In my view, the only legal basis a regulator can have to challenge commissions on personal consumption is to characterize the money paid for product purchases as money being paid for "head- hunting" or "paying to play." Another version of the same problem is the specific requirement in many laws that the company's plan be "primarily" about moving products and services to consumers, rather than about recruiting more "participants." But that issue brings us back to the same place, if the purchases are linked to recruiting, rather than to traditional marketplace supply and demand, then the money paid for the purchases will be deemed disguised "headhunting" fees. Now we are getting to the title: Are they worth it?

Nothing I have written above is new. The traditional methods of dealing with these concerns are the "ten customer rules", "90 percent buy back protection", and the "70 percent rule," derived from the 1979 Amway decision. These protections and techniques all have their good points. Yet some regulators view them as inadequate, or subject to manipulation, going so far as requiring company verification of independent representative submissions. The following is a different (and I believe, complementary) "test," attempting to focus more on substance than form.

Does the purchaser want/need the products or services and is the purchaser willing to buy them without the added incentive of an income opportunity?

The test is this: If the surrounding facts support the position that the goods are being purchased for their value, (Ask yourself - ARE THEY WORTH IT?) then the purchases are not being made as a "pay to play game." The facts must counter the regulatory accusation that, but for the income opportunity, no one would buy the products. I also suggest that the status of the purchaser (specifically, a total outside consumer or some form of independent representative) should make no difference.

I believe sales defined in this manner (which is one approach and not the only approach), directly addresses conduct that the anti-pyramid and endless chain laws seek to regulate. One way of stating the prohibited conduct is - the sale of products and services that no one will buy for their actual worth but will only buy to participate in and further an illegal endless chain. When such circumstances surround such sales, the sales become disguised headhunting fees, specifically prohibited by the laws of most states.

Would you buy your company's products, absent the income

opportunity? Would anyone? The answer needs to be "yes." If a company's sales are "primarily because the products are worth it" I believe the company can withstand legal scrutiny."

The Distributors

What Distributors say and do, can impact your company dramatically. If you don't believe this, then ask some of the many companies that have been brought down by a handful of rogue Distributors.

Distributors historically toe the line when it comes to how much risk they can bring to a company. Whatever a distributor does online without indicating that they are an "Independent Distributor", reflects on the company in a negative way, especially if it is non-compliant activities. Distributors often represent themselves as the company, they love to use online media, corporate URL's, and email addresses with the company name, perpetrating your trademarked brand; which creates unnecessary scrutiny and raises red flags to regulators.

Distributors can unknowingly put your company into a tailspin if enough of them are making income or drug claims about your product. Anything a distributor does or says reflects to your company brand.

The Executive Team

The Executive Team including the co-founders and owners can be a large exposure for the company. I have experienced owners who do not know how to tell their company story and/or product benefits without breaking their own policies by making drug and/or income claims.

When any member of the Executive Team acts as the face of the company, they must be impeccable with their speech about the company, the products, the compensation plan, the opportunity and the training. Owners don't get free passes out of compliance jail. What they say matters and is most often modeled by many of the upcoming Distributors.

Some executives tend to act as if they know everything, and do not budge even when proven wrong. They have a belief that focusing on compliance may hurt their company. It does not, I guarantee it.

Additionally, the Executive Team has a responsibility of supervising the Compliance Department. Lack of supervision can give a false sense of security to the Executive Team, thinking the Compliance Department is operating properly, but heaven forbid it is not.

Case Study: Herbalife
Contributed by Kevin Thompson, MLM Expert Attorney

In 2016, after a two-year investigation, Herbalife agreed to pay a $200 million fine to the FTC, and act in accordance with prescribed measures. With this announcement of a settlement, investors and proponents/opponents of the MLM industry alike are attempting to process what it all means for the Company's future. Before we provide you an in-depth analysis of the stipulations found within the FTC's Order for a Permanent Injunction and Monetary Judgment, it's important to remember that these prescribed actions only apply to Herbalife and not multi-level marketing companies collectively. In response to a question in which she was asked what kind of implications the settlement will have on the network marketing industry, FTC Chairwoman Edith Ramirez stayed mum on its long-term implications and stated rather plainly that the FTC would soon be providing additional guidance on legitimate network marketing companies. That aside let's get down to business, and clarify what the FTC's order does and does not say.

At the company level, 80% of Herbalife's revenue from product sales needs to be generated via a combination of retail sales and

"Rewardable" internal consumption. "Rewardable" is defined as a quantity less than $200 per month per distributor. The amount of "rewardable" internal consumption cannot comprise of more than 1/3rd of the total revenue, or else Herbalife is forced to reduce its payout by 10% (which basically works as a tax on the top earners).

This restriction is a bit odd. The formula is basically a strange way to ensure that 50% of the company's revenue comes via retail sales. And candidly, it's not the most problematic for Herbalife long-term. The public appears to be seizing on this 80% metric, thinking that Herbalife must cease operating if the 80% metric is missed. As explained above, the only penalty on Herbalife is a 10% reduction in what it can pay out. From the micro-perspective of an individual distributor, Herbalife in the future CANNOT pay any distributor who fails to have at least 66% of his or her total sales (personal and downline included) come from retail customers. Where am I getting this from? From the line in the Order that states, "Reward-able transactions (i.e., compensation) shall be limited such that no more than one-third of the total value of a participant may be attributed to [internal consumption] transactions."

If you will recall the restrictions imposed on Vemma, the FTC in conjunction with court approval currently allows Vemma to pay commissions to Distributors ONLY IF 51% percent of a distributor's downline sales originate from retail customers (I've previously referred to this as the "Vemma overlay'). I strongly suspected negotiations were stalling because the FTC wanted to impose Vemma-like restrictions... (I was right, BTW). Herbalife's restriction is more burdensome than the Vemma overlay. The FTC's limitation on allowable ("Rewardable") internal consumption mandates that a participant can only self-purchase: (i) no more than $200 worth of products per month for the first 12 months following the enactment of the Order; and (ii) post-twelve months of the Order's enactment, no more than the greater of EITHER $125 worth of products per month OR the calculated average amount of what three-fourths of Preferred Customers are buying over the previous twelve months. No more than one-third of a participant's compensation can originate from his/her personal consumption or the personal consumption of the downline.

As a continuation of its efforts to place the onus on Herbalife to acquire meaningful retail sales, the FTC put forth a very meaningful stipulation on rank and bonus qualification. To the extent that Herbalife requires its participants to meet any sort of target or threshold regarding rank advancement, bonuses, etc., a participant may only do so EXCLUSIVELY through retail sales. This is highly significant and illustrates the FTC's statement that Herbalife will "restructure [its] US business operations."

While only time will tell how Herbalife will choose to go about effectuating this particular stipulation, this sends a loud message that Distributors who are interested in climbing rank and thus becoming eligible to earn larger commissions must do so on the basis of their ability to generate customers and train downline members to do the same.

Some smaller but nonetheless important details from the Order deal with how the Company will track retail sales and its disengagement from certain industry norms. In order to verify retail activity, Herbalife must take "reasonable steps" that include "random and targeted audits." These audits will monitor retail sales and ensure sales occur in the manner in which they are reported. Speaking of such reporting, the Company will have to collect retail sale information from participants detailing: the method of payment; the product and quantities sold; the date; the price paid; first and last name of purchaser; contact information including information like telephone number or home address; and the signature of the Customer for any paper receipt.

Herbalife must discontinue practices commonly associated with network marketing companies. The Company can no longer require a participant to have a minimum quantity of products. Additionally, the FTC is outright banning Herbalife from providing participants with auto-ship, even an OPTIONAL auto ship. After what happened in Vemma, and now this, it appears safe to say that regulators greatly disapprove of personal volume quotas and auto ship requirements.

Just for the record, I called on the DSA 2 years ago to modify its Code of Ethics to prohibit companies from requiring monthly volume quotas (See item #2). The idea gets shot down whenever I bring it up. Regardless of the narrative spouted by companies, gravity naturally pulls Distributors to train other Distributors to simply "buy to qualify" i.e. "get on auto ship to stay qualified and recruit others to do the same." While there are other restrictions imposed by the order, the items referenced above are worthier of our time and study.

Largely hailed as a victory in the general media on account of the pyramid label omission, Herbalife faces significant challenges to its domestic survival. With participants now facing the requirement of having two-thirds of their sales originate from customers and the Company being required to operate with a pay plan that more closely resembles a Rubik's cube than an MLM pay plan, the FTC's game plan is crystal clear: (1) take money off the table today without firing a single shot ($200,000,000); and (2) force Herbalife to prove its legitimacy over the next several years. The FTC's avoidance of the pyramid label is very interesting and surprising. As I've said since January of 2013, the FTC has weak pyramid arguments against Herbalife. If they would have sued on that basis, they would have lost.

When it comes to prosecuting pyramid schemes, the current body of case law makes the FTC's job more difficult to impose its own vision of "fairness." Put another way, the FTC is not happy with the current state of the law. Instead of going down the pyramid road, the FTC is making a broader argument, stating simply that Herbalife's plan is likely to cause harm because it's inherently unfair.

What's an "inherently unfair" compensation plan? It appears the FTC is going to argue that an unfair pay plan primarily incentivizes recruitment over retailing. Did the FTC avoid the pyramid word by way of negotiations with Herbalife? Or was it done with specific intent to avoid the challenges associated with a pyramid argument? We'll find out soon enough. The FTC got a big bite at the apple. They got a lot of money up front. And they got Herbalife onto a different wrestling mat. Instead of alleging Herbalife to be a pyramid scheme, which would be like nailing Jell-O to a tree, the FTC can simply call upon this order in the future if Herbalife fails to comply.

It reminds me of the adage, "Good matadors never go after a fresh bull. They stick it a few times, let it bleed, then strike." Herbalife is going to bleed under these restrictions. But they'll honor the terms of the deal while focusing on their international operations. If they can scale those operations fast enough, the growth overseas will exceed the losses they'll likely face domestically. And who knows…. maybe Herbalife can thrive with this new model. We'll learn a lot in the next few quarterly reports.

What does this mean for the industry? Pay plans need to be revisited, sales cultures need to be re-trained and expectations need to be managed. Slow growth is the new fast growth."

The Compensation Plan

If you are thinking of opening a direct selling company, and you don't have a compensation plan yet, then you may want to seek out the instruction of a compensation plan expert developer. Plan on having an MLM expert attorney review and approve your compensation plan. It  is difficult to develop and verify your own plan, unless you are a mathematical whiz kid. I defer to those experts who create, test and tweak compensation plans. These compensation plan experts will save you time, money and late difficulty.

Whatever you do, don't wait to have them review your compensation plan. You must be open to the thought that your plan may not be perfect, and that it can use a few suggestions on how to make it legally sound. Listen to your attorney and play by the rules from the beginning. It will make life in the industry so much easier in the long run. Their job is to protect you, let them.

During the Needs Assessment performed with each new client, it is surprising to see that some companies do not even have their compensation plan in a long version, written out with definitions. Other companies have developed their own compensation plans from scratch and in some cases, compensation plans are borrowed from other companies. It is not smart to "borrow" another company's compensation plan. This can be extremely problematic since there is no initial knowledge of why the plan was developed, how the payouts were calculated, or how the plan even works.

Your compensation plan should be written in a narrative form with definitions so that your MLM expert Attorney can thoroughly review it in its simplest form. You should include all the graphs and charts necessary to explain the compensation plan in specific detail. The compensation plan blueprint should also include definitions for each term included in the compensation plan, such as what you call your Distributors, how they enroll customers and any requirements to earn commissions. Be sure to find someone that has developed more than a handful of compensation plans and is qualified to advise you of any required revisions. Please refer to the resources section of this book for my professional recommendation of an expert compensation plan developer.

The worst-case scenario would be your plan pays out too much which could result in the company falling victim to an untested plan. You never want to find yourself in the position of paying out too much in commissions because of programming errors. I recommend comprehensive Compensation Plan modeling to test the software well BEFORE you open the doors. Some plans have been modeled once the business is up and running; but this poses a more complex issue which is why you should consult with a compensation plan expert developer and software specialist in advance of rolling out the plan for the real-life test.

Do not let just anyone see your compensation plan until the final version is approved by an MLM expert attorney. As objective as they may promise to be, Distributors should not see your plan until it is finalized and approved by your expert MLM Attorney. No matter how hard they try; they may have a reason why they want to change your entire plan to the binary, manipulating it to their benefit, with them at the top to benefit the most.

Your compensation plan will require the proper legal disclaimers because a lack of one will alert regulators to the fact that it was never reviewed or approved by an MLM expert attorney.

Case Study: BurnLounge
Contributed by Kevin Thompson, MLM Expert Attorney:

"BurnLounge" was a purported network marketing company. They positioned themselves as a blend between iTunes, Myspace and Amway. The FTC filed its initial complaint against BurnLounge in June of 2007. After a bench trial (and a two-year wait), the judge held BurnLounge to be an illegal pyramid scheme.

It's important to understand the BurnLounge model for purposes of understanding the pyramid scheme analysis. Also, it's beneficial to understand the BurnLounge model because their failure is very informative for other companies in the network marketing space. At its core, BurnLounge created a network of replicated websites, referred to as "BurnPages." These BurnPages allowed the independent "retailers" (a/k/a Distributors) to sell music and other items. There were multiple entry points into the BurnLounge program:

- Retailer: Paid a $30 fee for the right to operate their own BurnPages. Retailers were not eligible to receive income from music sales. Instead, they received "Burn-Rewards," which they could redeem for music.
- Mogul: If they wanted to earn cash rewards, they had to pay $7 per month and purchase one of the product packages. Upon this occurrence, they were dubbed "Moguls.

The BurnLounge compensation plan is confusing. When referencing it, the judge wrote, "Indeed, it would appear that BurnLounge was attempting to create a labyrinth of obfuscation rather than a readily understood compensation system." Essentially, there were multiple income opportunities in the BurnLounge plan. There was a unilevel component where the participants earned a percentage of the volume generated by their personally enrolled representatives. In addition to this program, Moguls earned the "real money" in the binary plan. In order to qualify for the binary compensation, Moguls had to "sell" two VIP packages to members in their downline (the VIP package was the most expensive offering) and hit monthly performance standards. In the binary plan, Moguls earned a percentage of the total volume from their business by optimizing their two legs.

After waiting for two years after the trial, the judge finally concluded that BurnLounge was, in fact, a pyramid scheme. It's important for serious students of the network marketing industry should take a hard look at this case. There's a lot to be learned. In my opinion, if I were to point out one toxic element in their business model that ultimately led to the regulatory action, it would be the extra incentives in the compensation plan that led the majority of BL participants to buy the premium packages. The compensation plan drives behavior. When the barrier to the "real money" was the purchase of a premium package, the vast majority of participants will do it regardless if they really want the products. This appears to be the case with BurnLounge.

While BurnLounge tried hard to argue that its products were valuable, the extra incentives in the pay plan provided an easy opportunity for the FTC to argue that the participants bought the bundles to crack into bigger commissions. Simple mistakes led to big consequences."

Income Disclaimer

Income Disclaimer Example:

In the event that the company has not reached a year old, there may not be enough data available to complete a comprehensive Income Disclosure Statement. Whenever any income projection or representation is made publicly, it must be backed up by either the required Income Disclaimer or Income Disclosure Statement. Income projections or any representation of money requires the following robust Income Disclaimer (or very similar):

"There are no guarantees regarding income in the (company name) opportunity. The success or failure of each Independent Distributor, as in any other business, depends upon each Distributor's skills and personal effort. Earning levels for a (company's name) Independent Distributor that appear are just examples and should not be construed as typical or average. Income level achievements are dependent upon the individual distributor's business skills, personal ambition, time, commitment, activity, and demographic factors."

Income representations by Distributors are also represented by images; displaying large piles of money, fancy cars, expensive houses, and flashing big checks. Disclaimers must be clear and conspicuous as indicated in FTC 2013.com Disclosures - How to Make Effective Disclosures in Digital Advertising!

Income Disclosure Statements (IDS)

The Income Disclosure Statement is prepared after a company has been in business for at least 9-months to a year. Using the Income Disclosure Statement allows Distributors to make income claims; however, at the least, an Income Disclaimer should be used as the minimum when the IDS is pending or if there is no existing IDS.

The direct selling expert attorney and/or special consultant assists the company's CFO in preparing the IDS. Omission of the IDS will raise red flags, especially if the Distributors are making any income claims.

The IDS takes a considerable amount of time to compile in most cases because it is considered a legal document that is well worth the extensive development time; it must be done correctly in order for it to be utilized effectively. Creating the IDS requires strong Financial analysis skill and possibly sophisticated software to avoid any ambiguity and or mistakes.

Kevin Thompson is one of the premier attorneys in the direct sales industry. Founding member of Thompson Burton PLLC.; Kevin specializes in helping clients navigate regulatory complexities related to FTC compliance, government investigations, and litigation.

Kevin Thompson, MLM Expert Attorney, and Thompson Burton PLLC., contributed the following about the IDS:

"The best way for a company to ensure that claims regarding its payment plan are given properly is to put the information on a silver platter for the Distributors to use. It's not the Distributors' job to gather the data; it's the independent business owner's job to zealously represent your company and all the while properly disclosing the information provided to them. This is why every company should provide its Distributors with an income disclosure document: the ultimate, end-all-end-all, 'Swiss Army knife' for Distributors to give income claims."

Kevin further explains that at a minimum, an Income Disclosure Statement should include:

- A statement of the average amount of time per day, week or month spent by the Distributors at each rank to achieve the various levels;
- The year or years during which the disclosed results were achieved;
- A statement of the average earnings achieved by all Distributors at each rank;
- The highest and lowest earnings achieved weekly by Distributors at each rank; and
- The percentage of Distributors at each rank who achieve the average income.

It's time for the industry to wake up and smell the coffee. The FTC is taking these earnings claims very seriously. And as technology is making it simpler for Distributors to make these sorts of claims, the responsibility is increasing for companies to properly educate the field. Looking forward, it's vitally important to have adequate compliance training and to supply Distributors with the up-to-date information that they need to make proper income claims. Most importantly, the information needs to be provided in such a way that any consumer can look at the information and be able to understand the underlying facts so they may make a fully informed decision."

The Lack of Compliance Training
Contributed by Kevin Thompson, MLM Expert Attorney

> *"And as technology is making it simpler for Distributors to make these sorts of claims, the responsibility is increasing for companies to properly educate the field."*

It is not just having a Compliance Department and keeping track of violations that will keep a company out of trouble. A lack of compliance training will ultimately bring unnecessary attention from regulators and may be the downfall of the entire enterprise. The Federal Trade Commission has begun stating that companies must provide guidance and training to their Distributors. Other regulatory bodies have begun to consider whether or not direct selling companies are providing compliance training to every single distributor. As you will see in Chapter 8, there is much discussion for the need of specific compliance training for Distributors. It has everything to do with legal compliance education, testing, tracking, and accountability. One of the biggest regulatory risks is distributor compliance; it is difficult for a company to develop an adequate distributor compliance training system. Therefore, they do not develop sufficient training for Distributors, putting their company at risk for regulatory scrutiny."

The company is responsible for providing quality compliance education to the field. Period! If you don't provide quality education two things may happen:

1. Your Distributors may decide to invent their own training. This would be in rare cases but if that distributor was in a prior company that got shut down, they may be concerned about compliance enough to know lack of compliance training is problematic. The trouble with this notion is that distributor-based compliance training may not be compliant and will expose your company even more.

2. You can get your butt handed to you by an investigation into your company, especially if the discovery is that you knew the importance of compliance training but did nothing to ensure the field was properly aware of your compliance efforts.

Testimonials:

Ask any MLM expert attorney and they will tell you that testimonials represent a huge exposure for an MLM company. Distributors do not have any idea what is compliant when delivering a testimonial. A proper and compliant testimonial must be taught. As a matter of fact, customers can say anything, since they are not trying to get you to buy the product or succumb to the service,  as they have nothing to gain. Distributors, on the other hand must be careful since whatever they say can be construed as enticement and manipulation to purchase the product or service from them, which will come back on the company. Usually, testimonials being made about your product or service are way too long, and in most cases diminishing to the intended goal of powerfully promoting the company's product or service.

Social Media & Online Reputation Management

Direct selling companies must be familiar with ALL social media platforms as well as be concerned with how they can impact the company's online reputation. You would be foolish to think that your Distributors are not using social media to promote and sell your product. The Distributors may explain the compensation plan in detail and many times forget to use the disclaimers that can trigger a regulatory red flag. If Distributors are not taught how to do the right things when marketing the business online, they will not be very effective on social media, which can make you vulnerable and susceptible to a regulatory investigation.

Social Media represents a large risk and must be handled as such. There are social media experts that you can utilize to teach proper social media etiquette. I provided one such resource in the back of this book.

Social Media provides the perfect outlet for Distributors to post things they must not. Distributors make drug and income claims, they show pictures of piles of money, they attempt to solicit others from your organization or any company's organization to join their private Facebook page.

Distributors like to show off things that are meant for "Internal Use Only" or requires a back-office login - they like to show checks, cars, product lab tests and you name it. Whatever information the Distributors have access to, you are going to see again (it may even be modified from its original version and intended use) out on the Internet on any number of social media or self-created websites. This must be monitored and stopped as it happens.

Direct Selling Solutions as your outside Compliance Consultant, will assist you in the development of the company's Social Media and marketing guidelines based on your finalized and approved Policies and Procedures. DSS offers both manual and automatic systems for online social media monitoring, which is a major need for large scale companies.

Sales Literature and Marketing Materials
The Executive Team must consult with the direct selling expert

attorney for approval on all sales literature and marketing materials.

Sure, you may share a few of your marketing items with the attorney from the beginning and that is a start. However, as the company grows and the owners begin to think they know best about compliance, and without consulting a Compliance Consultant, they begin to take risks on flyers, PowerPoints, banners, compensation plan handouts, etc. Sometimes, the executives don't even know that they are taking a high risk, especially if marketing literature is producing sales like hotcakes.

Don't be apathetic on your compliance approval processes. As things change, run them by your attorney for review - safest bet. This is an excellent reason to have a direct selling expert attorney on retainer from the beginning.

Company approved sales literature and marketing materials are among the written documents considered evidence in an investigation. What does your sales literature and marketing materials say about your company, your compliance efforts? What does it say to intelligent people who recognize the potential legal risks of the materials? Viable prospects won't ask questions, they won't want to affiliate with  your company, they will just walk away, and you may never know why.

Use the attorney you retain; that is what they are on your team for. Listen to them they know what you need to do and should. If your MLM expert attorney is going to defend you in any investigation, they will need to know the big picture from the beginning and must be kept in the loop, ongoing.

PCI Compliance

What is PCI?

The Payment Card Industry Data Security Standard (PCI DSS) is a set of security standards designed to ensure that ALL companies accepting, processing, storing or transmitting credit card information maintain a secure data protection systems environment.

The Payment Card Industry Security Standards Council (PCI SSC) was launched on September 7, 2006 to manage the ongoing evolution of the Payment Card Industry (PCI) security standards with a focus on improving payment account security throughout the transaction process. The PCI DSS is administered and managed by the PCI SSC (www.pcisecuritystandards.org), an independent body that was created by the major payment card brands (Visa, MasterCard, American Express, Discover and JCB).

What are the penalties for non-compliance?

It is important to be familiar with your merchant account agreement, which should outline your exposure. The payment brands may, at their discretion, fine an acquiring bank $5,000 to $100,000 per month for PCI compliance violations. The banks will most likely pass this fine along until it eventually hits the merchant. Furthermore, the bank will also most likely either terminate your relationship or increase transaction fees. Penalties are not openly discussed nor widely publicized, but they can be catastrophic to a small business.

Merchant Account

You cannot do business without a merchant account and it may be necessary to have multiple accounts. Depending on how and with whom you set your merchant account up with, could result in your immediate need for a second merchant account. It is important for any company to maintain at least 2 to 3 merchant accounts, just in case.

The world of merchant accounts, historically, does not like the direct selling industry. If you happened to set up your merchant account with the bank, without them knowing you are in the direct selling industry, you may have trouble in the future. Merchant account processors must be told up front that you are working within the direct selling industry.

The recommendation, from merchant account experts, supports having more than one account and suggests actively using both accounts. It would not be unusual for a company to potentially double in size creating a sharp increase in money moving through the merchant account. The need for both accounts is that some merchant accounts cannot handle massive growth of a company within a short period of time.

If the merchant account provider does not do business with and did not know a company was operating in the direct selling industry, the account could be frozen without notice and the money will be put on indefinite reserve. When a merchant account funds are put on reserve or frozen for the first time, those funds may not be release for up to 6-months, if not more. The last thing anyone wants, or needs is to have their cash flow shut off with no real warning or explanation, which the merchant account provider surely has the right to do.

A couple of things that can radically affect a merchant account are chargebacks and not upholding PCI compliance. The chargebacks are somewhat easy to address if there is proof (in most cases). As unfair as this may sound, it is always best to give customers their money back if they are not happy. Unhappy customers chargeback sales without any warning, as well as complain to potential customers, to the consumer protection agency and even the Attorney General about your poor customer service and refusal to honor their request for a refund. It is best to and less hassle to just give them their money back and process refunds, immediately.

The PCI compliance requires that companies protect customer's credit card information at all times. One of the biggest problems for companies processing applications online, is that when signing someone up at a location without computer access Distributors tend to jot the potential Distributors information down on a paper application or worse write the credit card data on a napkin and carry it around with them increasing the risk of the prospect's data potentially being exposed publicly. The new Distributor sees the existing Distributor do this and repeats it when they sign someone up (learned behavior).

A distributor cannot keep credit card data handwritten on a piece of paper. Distributors cannot keep credit card data for any length of time. In some cases, a company will endorse or turn their head to this happening. Not smart. If the merchant account finds out this is what you are doing, your merchant account can be shut down due to failure to remain PCI compliant, and you may not ever get it back.

Do not gamble with having only one merchant account. Get approved ASAP for another one. Rotate the charges by day, such as Monday, Wednesday, and Friday. Rotate what gets processed and when. For example, run sales aid sales on one merchant account, run event registrations on another. Build the income into these accounts slowly and communicate with your merchant processor on any expected processing increases. You may choose to have four or five merchant accounts running at the same time. You may need seek out new processors. Do not get complacent if this is the case.

Third Party Websites (Distributor Produced)

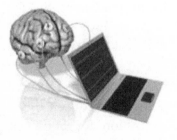

Anything online including a website is considered evidence. Whatever Distributors post online can be problematic. Therefore, so many companies do not allow their Distributors to even have third- party websites. The company does not have the time or resources to monitor independent distributor's third-party websites. Things to watch out for on websites are income claims, product or drug claims, use of unauthorized product videos, use of company logo instead of independent distributor logos, bad-mouthing other companies, misquoting the compensation plan, underpricing the product, and misrepresenting the product warranty. Compliance staff does not usually monitor third party websites. Even after the initial approval and authorization to publish, Distributors can change the site back to the non-compliant issues, representing a huge risk for the company.

Events:

Often the most easily accessible and preferred method for regulators to attend are public open Distributor and company events, anonymously. Regulators have been known to join the company as a Distributor so that they are able to hear conference calls, testimonials, and attend events auditing for regulatory  violations. Once you are in the crosshairs of a regulator, there is no doubt that they will join your company, the rest is a part of their basic investigation.

It is incredibly important to have your regional and annual events coordinated and audited often by the compliance team. Companies must be cautious when posting disclaimers for both incomes and products at their events that are always visible. The Compliance Department must screen all Distributors that are speaking at the event in advance, this includes reviewing scripts, PowerPoint slides and YouTube videos that have been developed by the Distributors and will be shared from the stage. The worst thing that can happen is that a distributor lays out a company promotion and slants it to be recruitment-based activities. Having a quality production company reduces this risk. Direct Selling Solutions offers full protection for both event preparation, presentations and video production. Events can also represent a high risk, simply by the sheer magnitude of the people in attendance sharing information in conversations.

Asset Protection and Wealth Preservation

Part of every owner's compliance preparedness plan should include a robust asset protection strategy. In the event of regulatory action, the owner, and even the owner's families' checking accounts, credit accounts, and other accounts may be seized. It is critical to have separate financial resources during these times. It would be beneficial to seek out an asset's protection expert attorney in order to protect those assets in case a regulatory infraction arises.

Chapter 3

DIRECT SELLING "SOLUTIONS" TO
COMPLIANCE MANAGEMENT SYSTEM (CMS)

Compliance Preparedness is the KEY!

SETTING up and running a healthy Compliance Department is an ongoing effort. When a department has been set up properly with full support from the owners, it has its best chance of success. Without a strong foundation, the department may be in for some difficulties later.

Successful implementation of the Compliance Management System (CMS) can build the foundation for the Compliance Department for many years to come. To have a productive Compliance Department, the company must incorporate the entire CMS into their business model with no exceptions. Utilizing the CMS system to its full potential ensures the company functions efficiently. When only bits or pieces of the System are utilized, the system loses its stability and becomes inefficient, whereby minimizing effectiveness. If ever under regulatory scrutiny, the CMS data will provide countless benefits.

Direct Selling Solutions has several, customizable options to name a few: a DIY option, a full-service option or a combination option for delivering our services. When you are ready, we are available immediately to serve as your Compliance Officer.

A Compliance Officer is a critical component to the department and responsible for several areas such as helping the company reduce regulatory risk, providing essential education for executive staff and Distributors, as well as providing the ongoing documentation, when needed. All of which ensures a level of protection and security for your company that is critical for its success. The Compliance Officer may be someone that you promote in-house to oversee these efforts. If someone on staff is not available to facilitate your compliance efforts, because some companies do not have the funds to bring on a full-time person to handle compliance responsibilities in the beginning; in those cases, Direct Selling Solutions steps in and works remotely (online) as the Compliance Officer (many client's preference).

There are several ways we work with clients to help them establish their Compliance Department, depending on budget and needs. First things first, let's look at the foundation of a company's current compliance efforts, then establish where your efforts need the most attention, develop a strategy and move forward from exactly where you are.

It's ALIVE!

The CMS is a moving, living, breathing system designed to grow with your company's needs. In the event a company has already had any regulatory inquiries, specialized forms may be created to track specific metrics as well as aid in the maintenance of data and the archiving of vital documentation for the company to provide to regulators.

The CMS is essential to your Compliance Department, but it's just the beginning. A well-functioning Compliance Management System will establish guidelines, uphold the Policies & Procedures, and always be under development. The CMS is your blueprint to success and literally establishes the foundation and record-keeping for your

Compliance efforts.

The system provides several generic logs that may be revised and customized for your company. The CMS also provides generic forms, checklists, templates for letters and much more. The system also includes a comprehensive job description for the Compliance Officer.

Whatever you decide to call your compliance staff person, the job description will outline their priorities. The job description will make you aware of what the expectations are for that position.

It is extremely beneficial for companies to have Direct Selling Solutions on board to hold your compliance staff accountable. DSS will contribute to the proper formation of your Compliance Department.

As your Compliance Department grows more and more sections of the CMS will developed and implemented. You must keep records of Distributor violations, so you will be able to track the offense occurrences as well as keep up with the sequence and frequency of notifications. When a Distributor has committed an offense, the probability of them offending again is very likely. Some people just want to see how much they can get away with before being discovered. Other will challenge the compliance decisions continuously to sway the system to their benefit.

The Marketing Policies at a Glance is a succinct view of what the company expects of their Distributors from a business marketing standpoint. The Marketing Policies at a Glance takes the entire Policy and Procedure document, reduces it to a one or two-page handout, allowing Distributors to learn about the Policies without having to read the entire 40+ page manual. This service is included in my first month of consulting, once retained.

It is the company's responsibility to know what your Distributors are saying about your products, your company, and your opportunity; therefore, making another ever-growing section of your CMS the testimonial section. Working with Distributors regularly from the start, teaching them how to deliver a powerful and compliant testimonial will save the company time and money.

Distributors must know how to discuss ALL aspects of the business and remain compliant which keeps everyone involved out of scrutiny from regulators and prospects. Correctly giving testimonials also gives the public positive notion that your company is aware and intolerant to such exposures.

Once we get the CMS up and rolling, the next step is the development of the Compliance Action Plan. This plan will allow you to determine the department budget, staffing and long/short-term goals. The Action Plan addresses an annual calendar that will assist owners/founders with getting the company Compliance Department up and running, effectively as well as allowing DSS to keep a magnified eye on the system's efforts and progression.

The executive team and I develop the Compliance Action Plan. We submit a first draft of the Plan and we formulate monthly goals and objectives for each area of compliance importance from there.

Documentation — Cover Your Ass "CYA"

One super, critical step involved in Compliance coordination for any Direct Selling company is documentation, documentation, and more documentation. You may not be a paperwork kind of person, but your Compliance Department person had better be. You want to be out building your business and making your brand known while your compliance person is working to keep your business safe. You want to be safe from federal, state, or local government intervention -and- heaven forbid it happens, the compliance documentation, if done properly, will undoubtedly CYA.

Your compliance person must be a detail-oriented, strong communicative person who has the skills to follow up with issues on a timely, firm and consistent basis. Compliance documentation is one of the most essential factors in the event of a regulatory investigation. Documentation provides evidence that your company has an effectively active Compliance Department.

Your Compliance Department will live and die by its documentation. Compliance documentation evidence is a priceless asset when you are faced with any regulatory investigation, or one triggered by an independent Distributor claiming their position was unwarrantedly terminated.

A well-balanced action plan blueprint for your Compliance Department provides important documentation in case of legal scrutiny.

Internally the Compliance Department documents:

- Inquiries, infractions, complaints to the Compliance Department.
- Requested authorizations and approvals from your MLM Expert attorney and company executives.
- Reports of unauthorized products and opportunity listings on Social Media.
- Possible actions Distributors may threaten to take against the company.
- Replies to inquiries into the department or company. Audits of company sponsored trainings, leadership meetings, and local or national events.
- Reports of income opportunity meetings and conference calls regarding Compliance.
- Documents of all correspondence from any regulatory entity and/or other attorneys.

Monitoring the Field is Part of the CMS: There is no substitution for Compliance monitoring, ever!

Auditing events - this is a must! If you have "The Compliance Department" visible at your events, questions can be answered on the spot and with authority. A bonus is educating the field on compliance requirements at meetings and events. Monkey see, monkey do. It starts at the top!

Monitoring the field ensures that Distributors do not make non-compliant representations. ALL public representations of the company from your Distributors carry the same weight as if the Owner or Founder stated them. In order to monitor the field, you need to observe events to ensure that Distributors are not making any false claims, and that they are not sharing misleading information about your company, products, services or the opportunity.

Showing up at the event is also a good way for the Distributors to meet the compliance team. When individuals know that the compliance department is possibly going to be present at their events, they tend to be more certain to follow the guidelines set for them by the company. A few examples of some of the events that must be monitored and documented randomly are:

- Conference Calls
- Trainings, in person and digitally
- Annual and Regional company sponsored events
  Opportunity Meetings
- Super Saturday Trainings
- Special events such as company sponsored fund raising, PR or Media involvements
- Incentive trips - do Compliance training at them! Tradeshow requests

An Internal Compliance Department is responsible for the above and so much more. Performing consistent monitoring and enforcement is a requirement. It is detrimental for a company to have ZERO history of compliance enforcement, the results can be devastating.

Auditing and monitoring field compliance is vital. This includes monitoring field opportunity meetings randomly. The Compliance efforts must start at the top. If an owner or founder is not willing to have a compliance person audit any event, they must have their head in the sand; there is no excuse for obliviousness in a compliance situation!

One way that regulators get the real scoop on a company they may be looking at is to attend their events. It's easy, all they must do is join as a customer or a Distributor and plug in. They listen and record YOUR conference calls to be used against you in future. They attend your events. PERIOD, over and out - if you (as an owner) stand up and give unsubstantiated claims about your products, they've gotcha, and most likely on tape!

The Compliance Department should be consulted from planning to implementation of the event. Your compliance professional is or should be a respected core member of the event planning and production process. Providing a high level of compliance involvement when moving forward with events helps to indicate that you are operating your company with monitored compliance practices.

Chapter 4

GATHERING THE COMPLIANCE TEAM

When to Bring on a Direct Selling Expert Attorney

THINK ABOUT THIS, why would you go to a doctor specializing in the removal of your appendix, when who you REALLY needed was a Cardiologist? So, why do so many companies think that their sister's husband, a divorce attorney, can help set up a legally sound direct selling company?

I've been in this industry since 1991. I have had the liberty of seeing the good, the bad, and the ugly. When it gets ugly, it is too late to call in the lawyers and when it is too late to call in the lawyers - the legal dealings will get expensive, really fast.

In my opinion, direct selling companies require an expert MLM attorney right from the beginning. The wise counsel of an expert in the field will save you thousands and, in some cases, can literally keep you out of jail.

I ask new owners, and some existing owners – if they have ever visited a Federal Penitentiary? Why would anyone risk the money, their company, and potentially their freedom? Consult with an expert right off the bat, to avoid any of these possible outcomes.

When retaining an MLM expert attorney be positive that they have previous experience in the direct selling industry. An inexperienced attorney typically lacks a fundamental background with direct selling documentation. For example, if the company chooses to employ their cousin, the divorce Attorney, or the real estate Attorney to help in the formation of their Direct Selling company it may fail, and quickly. When a company chooses not to use an MLM Expert Attorney, but instead relies on an inexperienced (non-MLM experienced) attorney, the company can literally run out of money due to legal expenses incurred by the mistakes of that Real Estate Attorney.

There is no retracing your footsteps once you start your company with an inexperienced attorney. The type of mistakes that can be made would compound to be problematic beyond your fears.

Some small startup companies whether they work from their homes or have nice big offices, may not realize they need legal advice until it is a little too late. Some only call the experts in when they have received a letter from a regulatory entity or a letter saying they owe a fortune in sales tax and fines or that they have regulatory issues.

If you hesitate for even a minute in your reply to respond to a threatening Distributor, call your direct selling expert attorney before you send a reply. It is important to keep a written (digital) record of the interaction. The Attorney will ask for a history on the case. If your Compliance Department keeps those records consistently, it makes for easy retrieval of the facts, if needed.

It would be smart to have a direct selling expert attorney on retainer to double-check your marketing materials and your compensation plan. Double check any questionable incentives or contests you design; some may be considered recruitment based instead of customer based. Have a sales volume requirement to the contest, it keeps the company at a lower exposure level and any time a company can avoid these red flags is a plus. Some of what the expert attorney will do:

- Your expert MLM attorney reviews and authorizes compensation plans.
- The attorney must be able and willing to defend the compensation plan if any regulatory issues present themselves.
- In a new startup company, the MLM Expert Attorney should be hired prior to doing extensive planning of your compensation plan and soft- ware development.
- The most important thing an Expert Attorney will provide is an extensive evaluation of the compensation plan in development PRIOR to your authorizing your software vendor to start programming. Do not share your compensation plan with your software vendor prior to your Expert Attorney's review. Any revisions required by your Expert Attorney would have to be reprogrammed and can be very costly.

A Policies and Procedures document can is one of the things that you will need expert assistance with and can be as long as 25-40+ pages long and the MLM expert attorneys know exactly what has to go into this document for this industry and for your type of company, keeping you in good legal standing with MLM Regulators. What may appear to be a cheaper alternative can be stressful, time-consuming and extremely costly of both time and money, in the long run. An Expert Attorney will generally provide the following documents that they or you customize for your company:

- They should review and comment on the proposed company compensation plan PRIOR to programming with your software vendor
- The draft of the company Policies and Procedures
- The Independent Distributor application and agreement Term and Conditions of the Independent Distributor relationship
- The customer order form
- The refund policy
- The online customer sign-up process
- The Privacy Agreement
- The auto ship text
- Additional documentation as required

When the client requests it, the MLM expert attorney will provide their legal opinion letter. These letters can be lengthy and be an additional charge. It's a good thing to have, kind of like insurance that your attorney can defend the company based on the information they discovered when preparing the letter of opinion.

It would be beneficial for your expert attorney to review company-developed YouTube videos. Especially in cases where you are going to release a video at a company sponsored event. Double-check your YouTube video for compliance instead of providing a regulator with ammunition about your program because of the red flags that your videos contain.

MLM expert attorneys teach you how to build a solid legal foundation for your company. Listen to them.

Working with Your Compliance Consultant

Now you've read about the importance of the Compliance Department, you might be thinking, 'I don't want to mess with all this compliance stuff. I just want to grow my business.'

Work your strengths, delegate your weaknesses, and inspect your delegations. As a successful business owner, I'm sure you've learned over time one of the best ways to get work completed you don't want to do yourself is to delegate. Delegating will prove you need assistance and aid in getting the job done quickly and accurately.

Your compliance needs can be addressed by utilizing an outside consultant who is more effective and experienced than an internal staff person. This will strengthen your ability of your business to keep running without legal interference.

An outside consulting arm such as Direct Selling Solutions, (operating in Direct Selling Compliance since 1991), may provide compliance training to your staff and your leading Distributors. This compliance training will begin the learning process and get the Distributors familiar with the regulatory guidelines, reviews, audits, and monitoring keeping your company stable, compliant, and profitable.

As an outside consultant, I offer my clients the proprietary Compliance Management System (CMS). It includes necessary forms, checklists, sample letters, templates for forms, and many other resources to establish an effective and efficient Compliance Department within their direct selling company. The CMS is a huge time and money saver as compared to any competitive sources.

When we work with a client, we offer them 25+ template letters to address compliance issues. In many cases, since there are some basic violations that will keep coming up, they will only use 4 or 5 of the letters. Just be sure to run termination letters by your Direct Selling Expert Attorney before you send them out, as they may become larger issues if not handled tactfully.

Included in this material are two warnings, one suspension and one termination template. In some case, it is beneficial for the Distributor to receive an Acknowledgement document stating they understand they were in violation of your Policies and face immediate termination if any more offenses occur. The process and decisions must be made based on the owner's desire and the company's culture on how they handle compliance correspondence and/or the number of violations this Distributor has been notified of, already.

It will be very important for your Expert Attorney to review the types of letters you are sending most often and to sign off on ALL your self-developed templates. There is an attorney submission process included later in this material if you do not currently have one. Direct Selling Solutions works directly with the most respected attorneys in the industry.

It is important to stay in compliance before regulators knock on the door. Using the Direct Selling Solutions master intake process, your Compliance Department can easily track compliance inquiries, violations, results and follow-up.

Direct Selling Solutions provides the set-up protocols and for opening and running your Compliance Department. The Compliance Management System (CMS) provides checklists for opening and running the Compliance Department, master intake process, Internet activities processes, forms, and template letters used for warning, suspending, or terminating a Distributor, when necessary.

Direct Selling Solutions becomes immediately familiar with the company Policies & Procedures and any pending issues. All incoming compliance reports, complaints or issues are immediately brought to my attention through the company's compliance email. We then take that incoming information and set up an intake process to document each incident individually. We coordinate with a staff person on a daily or weekly basis to bring the company up to date on any current demanding compliance issues. Direct Selling Solutions monitors both company leading Distributors and problem Distributors daily to track and monitor their online activity.

When necessary, we provide a compliance update report so the Customer Service Supervisor, the VP of Sales, the Marketing Team, the Operations Supervisor, the Founder/Owner will be kept up to date on compliance issues (if they are actively involved in Distributor activities).

Another way we work with clients is to provide support to their current compliance staff. This support may include setting up the necessary forms, checklists, and necessary correspondence. We sometimes find one customer service staff person generally runs Compliance Department. Most customer service staff do NOT have the experience necessary to handle the Compliance Department efficiently and effectively on their own without a blueprint such as the CMS or direct supervision.

Sometimes, the company requests that we train someone to handle the compliance responsibilities down the road. Direct Selling Solutions assists in the selection process and provides the necessary training (when the person has a base of compliance education and/or network marketing experience). Working together we then develop a customized job description for the Compliance Officer to identify the vital areas of responsibility for their new position. It can take anywhere from three to six months to teach someone how to handle a fully operating Compliance Department, once trained, Direct Selling Solutions will continue in a supervisory role.

Finding the RIGHT Compliance Officer

Where to start?
- First things first, who do you know?

- Whose desk does your company's compliance issues land on, currently?

- Who is handling callers who are upset, frustrated and angry about your Policies and Procedures?

- Who is monitoring internal policies about field compliance?

It is important to have the right person in the position of Compliance Officer. The wrong person may cause your company irreversible harm. Make wise choices. Don't be afraid to cut an unqualified person from the Department. Eventually, it will save you money and frustration.

Let's start with the people who will be running the Compliance Department.

You will need someone you can trust, someone with letter writing skills, with great follow up and follow through skills to run the department. First, let's look at the current talent to pull from within the company. Is there an obvious choice?

Not Recommended as Compliance Officer:
- The Founder
- The Owner
- Spouse of Owner or founder
- Current President or VP of any department
- Master Distributor
- The Shipping Clerk

So many times, we learn the person selected by the owner to be the Compliance Officer is fits in one of the above categories. Under almost all circumstances the above people do not make good Compliance Officers nor support your company's compliance department operations which is vital to the long-term success of your company. An experienced professional Compliance Consultant such as the team at Direct Selling Solutions must monitor the person you choose.

Input from the owner or founder is imperative to having a successful Department. This Department provides needed evidence in case of any regulatory investigation. You, as the owner or founder, must have knowledge of key aspects of a Compliance Department, but not the minute details of the operation. It really does start at the top with compliance. Whomever you put in place, as your Compliance Officer will need to have a strong personality because, there may be times they'll have to rein you in and remind you to stop making inappropriate claims about your company and/or products.

Over the years, I've discovered trouble generally starts at the top with the Master Distributor, the leading Distributors, and/or the Owner of the business. The Owner, Founder, or Master Distributor is usually the one mouthpiece and messenger of the company. If unsubstantiated claims or other false information is getting out to the field in error, most often it is one of those folks doing it. The team will repeat whatever claims, quotes, or tag lines the owner puts in place. It almost always starts at the top.

In some cases, you can listen to what is being said and follow it right up the chain to a leader saying it. This is so important because misinformation can circulate faster than the common cold in direct selling.

Whatever gets said is duplicated throughout the team, whether it's the staff, the leadership team or just the newest Distributor on the team. The wrong information can be shared by anyone in an electronic format that can put your company at major risk. By bringing an experienced team in to run your Compliance Department you will get the protection you need. Direct Selling Solutions can make a difference in assisting you to find the right Compliance Officer and potentially keep your business out of legal hot water.

Who is qualified to be your Compliance Officer?

Ask yourself, who would be the best fit for the Compliance Officer for your company?

- Who has excellent follow up skills?
- Who is calm, professional, and objective?
- Who can keep quiet about private and confidential matters?
- Who can write a letter and take notes on department

activities and has excellent documentation skills?
- Who knows how to build agendas and take minutes of important meetings?
- Who will not be influenced by the field leaders when it comes to important decisions?
- Who has a firm knowledge of your Policies and Procedures?
- Who may be well known in the field for being fair and professional?

As you can tell, this key person must have a professional attitude, be a good judge of character, keep things confidential and be a detail-oriented person; to work effectively in the Compliance Department.

The Compliance Department is only as effective as the integrity of the people who are in charge from the top down. Anyone can follow the rules, but it is the team who will affect change, who will build the culture while protecting the brand and who will uphold the Policies and Procedures of the company.

A significant factor of the CMS is having qualified people in place who have a commitment to maintain high ethical standards and will protect your company's reputation. Using this system will assist in the selection of the best person as your Compliance Officer. The direction of your company's Officer will solidify the efforts of your staff and Distributors. Everyone will be aware of the  "rules" and informed as to how to benefit from playing by those "rules." If you cannot find an experienced professional, you may have to cultivate someone into the responsibilities of Compliance Officer from within your company or even bring in a qualified person to handle the department. Skills to Qualify as a Compliance Officer

It is recommended a Compliance Officer be put in place to assist in the management the company's Compliance Department using the

Compliance Management System (CMS).

The CMS provides a job description in the Compliance Manual. It is a lofty description but a necessary one. Providing the tasks outlined in the description will take supervision and organization to keep all required documents in order on an ongoing basis.

Ultimately, your Compliance Officer has your company Compliance efforts in their hands. They will set the tone for your Department. Hiring a Compliance Officer is as important as selecting a Nanny for your small children. Have specific guidelines for hiring. Verify all application information and the applicant's intention to be vigilant in overseeing the Compliance Department.

Your Compliance Officer can be your best resource in the case of a regulatory investigation. These characteristics are needed in the Compliance Officer:

- *Experience.* Be experienced in the legal compliance industry or have more than one year at their current company in customer service. Have an excellent work and attendance history at his/her company.
- *Computer skills.* Be proficient in Excel, Google
- *Docs/Sheets, and Zoom.* If not, they should at least be willing to learn.
- *Communication skills.* Can write letters, computer correspondence, newsletter articles, reports and communicate effectively and compassionately with the entire team of staff and Distributors.
- *Investigation skills.* Must be able to listen to facts objectively, delve into the details of an investigation, report it, and implement sanctions if necessary, on a consistent basis.
- *Social Media skills.* Can communicate on social media, Facebook, emails, and other social media platforms.
- *Confidentiality skills.* Must keep information from and about the company and the Compliance Department confidential under all circumstances.

- *Documentation skills.* Must keep detailed daily reports regarding infractions, suspensions, and terminations; as well as records of contacts with people within and outside of the company. Reporting skills are critical.
- *Teaching skills.* Have confidence and the ability to present information to the top leaders and Distributors at company sponsored events and trainings.

What Does the Compliance Officer Do?

Again, your Compliance Officer documents everything coming in and out of the department nonstop. It is a critical component of the Compliance Department. Anything that has a bearing on the matter at hand must be documented and stored for easy retrieval.

The Compliance Officer:

- Protects the customers, the Distributors, the product, the company, the brand and the owners
- Take the burden of Compliance Management from the owner and/or founder
- Works closely with Distributors when concerned about the company Policies & Procedures and potential violations. Addresses infractions in writing
- Monitors social media and the field documents for possible infractions in the CMS
- Reviews sales aids, literature, and marketing materials prior to release to the field by corporate or by any Distributors
- Corresponds with Distributors regarding violations and sanctions
- Coordinates and implements the compliance training efforts for the company Audits company events.

In summary the Compliance Officer is the gatekeeper for your business and ensures your Leadership team and Distributors have all the tools, training and compliance information necessary to stay out of FTC crosshairs.

Chapter 5

HOW TO SET UP, DOCUMENT AND TRACK YOUR COMPLIANCE DEPARTMENT

The Compliance Management System (CMS)

THE CMS INCLUDES forms and letter templates to assist in setting up your Compliance Department. The forms provided may be used as is or may be customized for your company. Some situations warrant more edits than others. Since the forms are available in WORD or EXCEL files, it is easy to modify as necessary.

An effective Compliance Department utilizes a variety of letters and can benefit from utilizing well thought out forms that provide structure for the department. The CMS has assembled over 30 template letters that have been used to address many different distributor issues. The letters include warnings, suspensions, and terminations, as well as templates to address Facebook, online sales, cross sponsorship, and other generic

Business Letter Format

Your Street Address
Your City, State Zip
Date

Heading

Inside Address

First and Last Name of the Person to whom you are writing
Their Street Address
City, ST Zip

Salutation   Body

Dear Mr./Ms. Full Name:

You do not want to indent when you are using this format. This is the best format to use when you are writing a persuasive letter. You want to introduce yourself and the topic you are writing about to the reader. Remember that the first rule of writing is to know your audience. In a persuasive letter, you state your opinion or your feelings about something that is important to you after you have introduced yourself. You must sound as professional and passionate as possible. You do not want to belittle the reader or they will not finish reading your letter. Your letter needs to have the facts, reasons, and examples to support your position. Address issues that your reader may have in their argument.

In a second paragraph, you must have solutions. Without solutions, you are only complaining. Offer assistance in solving the problem. Remind the reader where they can contact you.

Sincerely yours,

Signature

A. Student

infractions. These templates can be modified and used in a variety of situations.

Professional Template Letters

The Compliance Management System includes letters that make managing the department more efficient and provide the documentation necessary to support the company. Included in the full CMS are samples of over 30 professional template letters. The key to using these letters is to associate the infraction to a specific policy number and explain why the company believes the policy was violated. The sample letters listed below indicate what disciplinary actions the company may take if the infraction should continue. Again, these are sample letters and should be customized based on the company's policies. These letters may be emailed or sent via US Postal office (certified returned receipt).

All termination letters should be sent via US Postal office (certified returned receipt). If in another country, either send to the country manager (if one is in place) or send return receipt requested by email.

The acknowledgment form is used when either a second warning or a suspension letter is sent. If the violation warrants an acknowledgment it should be used. We find that when a distributor acknowledges their error, they have a lesser chance of violating again. Only in some cases do they sign the form and continue to violate the Policies and Procedures.

Listed below we have provided the various templates for letters regarding the stages of due process and of disciplinary action against Distributors.

COURTESY COMPLIANCE LETTER   0091

The Courtesy Compliance reminder or letter is used when a soft touch is needed. Maybe you just implemented a new policy and you don't want to slam a hammer on your distributors head. Depending on the severity of the offense, you may skip the courtesy reminder and move right to the First (1st) Warning letter.

Your Company Logo

(Date)

RE: Courtesy Compliance Reminder for <Insert Name and ID>

Dear <Insert Name>:

Thank you for your support and enthusiasm in spreading the word about our company and our products. We appreciate your excitement regarding our opportunity. You may not be aware that we have a policy regarding <insert issue>. We would like to share this courtesy reminder that <insert potential violation> is prohibited.

This type of infraction could be taken as a direct violation of your Distributor Agreement, which you accepted at the time of your application to <insert Company name>. In the event that these practices continue, <insert Company name> may take disciplinary action as outlined in the Company Policies and Procedures, which may include a warning or a suspension.

We appreciate all you do to share our vision. We wish you much success in building a profitable and long-lasting business with us.

Thank you in anticipation of your quick action regarding this matter.

Best regards,

<Insert Full Name>

<Insert Title>

<Insert Company Name>

OR

The <Insert Company Name> Legal Team

--------------------PRIVACY--------------------

This email transmission is confidential, privileged, and should only be read or stored by the intended recipient. If the reader of this program is not the intended recipient, you are hereby notified that any distribution or copying of this document is strictly prohibited. If you received this transfer by mistake, immediately notify the send and remove it from your system. Thank you.

FIRST WARNING LETTER 0092

The First (1st) Warning letter is your next stop after the Courtesy letter. This is used to notify distributors of failure to correct violation(s) stated in the Courtesy Compliance letter.

Your Company Logo

(Date)

RE: <Insert Distributor Name and ID #> Official Warning: <insert reason>

Dear <Insert Distributor Name>:

We appreciate your continued support and involvement with <insert Company name>. This serves as our 2nd attempt to notify you of a violation to your Distributor Agreement due to non-compliance with our Policies and Procedures (1st attempt was on <insert date>).

As per <insert Company name> Policies and Procedures, <insert section number of Policies and Procedures>...

<insert actual Policy pertaining to the violation>

Please take immediate action within 72 hours to be sure to keep your Distributorship in good standing.

You are invited to make a response to these allegations. You may be required to submit a signed statement of acknowledgment regarding this manner. Your response will be taken into consideration before <insert Company name> takes final action.

If no action is taken a compliance block may be placed on your account and the account may be considered for suspension or even permanent termination.

Please take the following action:

<list required actions>

<Insert Company name> will continue to monitor all Distributors, in accordance with the Policies and Procedures to ensure compliance with ethical business practices.

Your cooperation is greatly appreciated in this matter.

Best regards,

<Insert Full Name>

<Insert Title>

<Insert Company Name> OR

The <Insert Company Name> Legal Team

--------------------PRIVACY--------------------

This email transmission is confidential, privileged, and should only be read or stored by the intended recipient. If the reader of this program is not the intended recipient, you are hereby notified that any distribution or copying of this document is strictly prohibited. If you received this transfer by mistake, immediately notify the send and remove it from your system. Thank you.

ACKNOWLEDGMENT LETTER 1101

The Acknowledgment is a powerful tool. Never hesitate to have the distributor execute an acknowledgment. You may have to edit the four points and add or subtract to the document. Be sure to spell out the exact items that the company will be monitoring due to this situation.

(Date)

\<Insert full name & ID #>

Acknowledgment

This acknowledgment will act as the final warning regarding \<insert violation> that is visible on \<insert location/link>. Your use of \<insert violation> is non-compliant with the Policies and Procedures. The violation may jeopardize the future of \<insert Company name> and may increase likelihood of evaluation by regulators.

In order for you to maintain your active status as an Independent Distributor we require you to read, acknowledge, and abide by the following:

1. I am acknowledging that I have participated in non-compliant activities and that I will no longer continue any non-compliant activities going forward;

2. I acknowledge that I have read the current \<insert Company name> Policies and Procedures;

3. I acknowledge and agree to _____

4. I acknowledge that if I participate further in any violations that I may be subject to an **automatic termination**.

By signing this I acknowledge and will abide by the above statements

Print Name	ID #	Date

Signature	Witness

State of _____, County of _____

Subscribed and sworn to (or affirmed) before me on this _____ day of _____, 20 __, by _____, proved to me on this basis of satisfactory evidence to be the person(s) who appeared before me.

_____

Signature of Notary Public

SUSPENSION LETTER   0094

The Suspension letter is used to notify distributors of suspension from the company. This letter can be sent by email. To ensure that the distributor is properly notified, mail a hard copy if necessary.

Your Company Logo

(DATE)

RE: \<insert Distributor name & ID #\> **Suspension**

Dear \<insert Distributor name\>,

It has been brought to our attention that you have not made the necessary changes regarding \<insert policy violation\>.

Since you have not taken the required action, we must inform you that your Independent Distributor status has been SUSPENDED and you will not have access to your back office during this suspension period.

This suspension shall remain in effect until \<insert Company name\> has had an opportunity to thoroughly investigate the circumstances. Once the facts are collected, \<insert Company name\> will decide whether to reinstate your status, impose fines or terminate based on the severity of the infractions.

If you would like to submit a written statement to our Compliance Office, please do so within 3-days, which will then be taken into consideration.

OR

We will require a formal Acknowledgment to be completed and returned to compliance@company by you within 72 hours.

If new information is presented that exonerates or better explains your behavior, \<insert Company name\> will certainly take it into consideration.

In addition, if you do not correct your behavior \<insert Company name\> reserves the right to terminate your status as an \<insert Company name\> Independent Distributor.

Please conduct yourself accordingly.

Sincerely,

\<insert full name\>

Compliance Officer
\<insert Company name\>

--------------------PRIVACY--------------------

This email transmission is confidential, privileged, and should only be read or stored by the intended recipient. If the reader of this program is not the intended recipient, you are hereby notified that any distribution or copying of this document is strictly prohibited. If you received this transfer by mistake, immediately notify the send and remove it from your system. Thank you.

TERMINATION LETTER   0095

The Termination letter is used to notify distributors of termination from the company. This letter should be sent by mail with a return receipt or US Post Office Certified--return receipt mailed to ensure that the distributor is properly notified.

Your Company Logo

(Date)

\<Name of Distributor\>

\<Address\>

\<City, State, Zip\>

RE:\< insert Distributor name & ID#\> **TERMINATION LETTER**

Dear \<insert Distributor name\>,

On behalf of \<insert Company name\> your Distributorship with \<insert Company name \> is terminated effective immediately. You have been previously notified that you violated \<insert title of Policy\> of the \<insert Company name\> Policies and Procedures.

\<Insert BRIEF Distributor violation(s)\>

Our investigation has confirmed your unethical business activities. These activities violated the Policies and Procedures of \<Insert Company\>

You are no longer permitted to attend any \<insert Company name\> events or be involved in any \<insert Company name\> activities, including contacting \<insert Company name\> employees or Distributors related to any \<insert Company name\> affairs.

(If necessary, insert the following...) Please note that we reserve the right to press civil or criminal charges.

Act Accordingly,

\<insert full name\>

\<insert title\>

\<insert Company name\>

--------------------PRIVACY--------------------

This email transmission is confidential, privileged, and should only be read or stored by the intended recipient. If the reader of this program is not the intended recipient, you are hereby notified that any distribution or copying of this document is strictly prohibited. If you received this transfer by mistake, immediately notify the send and remove it from your system. Thank you.

The Compliance Flow Chart

Having a good working compliance notifications flow will assist in the development of systems, staff and responses. The chart on the following page diagrams the flow of an incident or alleged violation into the department from start to termination.

This example takes the violation through the process of intake, documentation, investigation, corrective action and alerting both the up line and a supervisor, if necessary. Each company can customize the flow based on their needs and culture.

This chart is based on years of experience that Direct Selling Solutions has working directly with, witnessed to, or consulted for - in dealing with regulatory investigations. This document provides the recommended structure and the required documentation for a compelling Compliance Department. It is the responsibility of the company and the Compliance Department to ensure these SOPs are followed consistently, regularly and without prejudice.

The documentation process starts as soon as the violation is discovered or reported. So think of it in two stages, the investigation stage and the due-process stage. The compliance action flow includes:

- potential infraction
- report to compliance
- verify infraction
- notification (1st contact)
- formal documentation begins – alerts
- corrected – yes or no
  - o Yes action-Thank you
  - o No action process continues
- No action
- 2nd warning – and determining action(s)

Compliance Flow

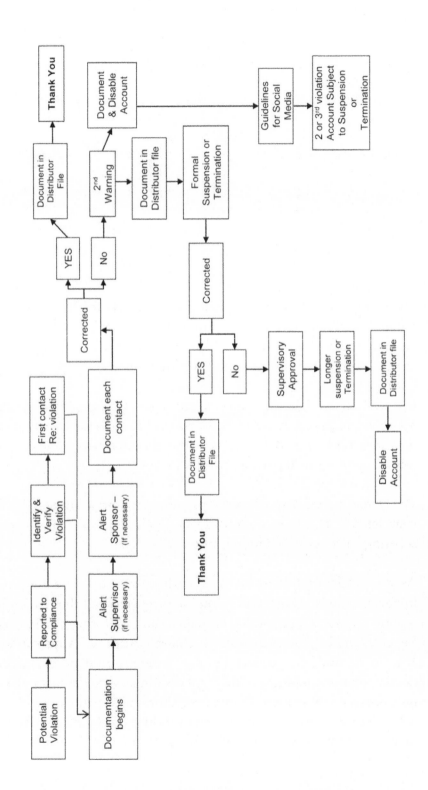

Action Plan: Compliance Goals

Compliance Department Setup

The Compliance Department Setup Checklist is to be used for initial Compliance Department foundation. It should also be used on an annual basis to ensure all documents have a current approval from the company's MLM Expert Attorney.

In addition to helping you ensure your Expert Attorney has approved all key elements of the company business (documentation, websites, marketing materials, etc.), this checklist also guides you in setting up files the department will utilize.

The Department Setup Checklist provides for important tasks to be completed BEFORE opening the Department. Each is a vital step in securing a proper foundation is put in place.

As you collect each item on the checklist, enter the date and your initials on the checklist. Once you have collected all the items that require attorney approval, complete an Attorney Approval Request, and log the request on the Master Attorney Approval log. You will find by collecting the proper written or digital documentation that some of the legal documents are missing or have never been put in place. Be sure to coordinate all documents with the MLM Expert Attorney. Be sure the product labels and marketing materials have been vetted BEFORE they are put into use. Keep written approval emails or letters from your MLM Expert Attorney for your files.

Compliance Department Ongoing Responsibilities

A checklist can remind a Compliance Officer to perform certain, required tasks to keep the Department running success- fully. A checklist provides for daily, weekly, monthly, and annual tasks. Each item has very specific reasons for being included on the checklist.

Perform all steps in a routine manner. Your Compliance Officer should have full authority to perform the actions included on the checklists. Many company owners or founders feel that one task or another is not necessary. Be sure to use the entire CMS as written. Do not be afraid to customize letters and create documents in order to contribute to the success of the department. Proper documentation is essential to running an effective Compliance Department.

One required task in setting up the Compliance Department is to seek the approval of your Policies & Procedures, and forms by an expert attorney. It helps ensure the company is free of compliance issues related to legal documentation and establishes the regulatory foundation of the Compliance Department. The absence of approved company documents can lead to serious allegations against the company, and in extreme cases, can result in penalties, or fines.

Legal documentation written by the MLM Expert Attorney should still be logged on the Compliance Department Setup Checklist so there is a record of the most recent approved documentation. Otherwise, all the elements listed on the checklist for attorney approval should be collected and sent to him/her for approval. The attorney approval process can be costly if your MLM Expert Attorney charges by the hour. If the attorney is on retainer, it shouldn't be a problem. In all cases supervisory or company owner permission should be sought before sending any documentation to the attorney.

Even if your Compliance Department is virtual, you will still need to have access to the working logs and additional documents. Google Sheets is a great way to keep on top of the required documentation and Intake Logs. Google Sheets allows you and your Compliance team to work in real time on the shared documents.

Two vital processes involved in the Compliance Department are the Master Intake Process and the attorney approval process. Those are foundational piece of this system and must not be left out.

Tracking the Department

The CMS is a proprietary system designed exclusively for the Direct Selling industry used to set up and maintain an effective Compliance Department. Set up an actual location in the office to keep the Compliance support documentation. ALL owners and founders need to know where these files are in case, they are needed for quick access.

Forms, Forms, and more Forms
Attorney Approval Request Process

The Master Attorney Approval Process is used to track items submitted to your MLM Expert Attorney. Use the Attorney Approval Request form to create individual  requests. It is recommended you set up a numbering system for requests to easily track and recall them quickly and efficiently. Most Compliance Departments use some combination of the year and request number. For example, 17-01 or 2017 01 refers to the first request logged in 2017.

The Attorney Approval Request form provides your attorney with all the details regarding any item requiring an attorney approval.

Provide as much detail as possible and attach the item to be approved. Of course, your attorney must vet all of your legal documentation.

Once you have all your operating documents approved by your attorney, you may decide to ask for approval for Distributor created marketing items. Your Compliance Department will be accepting requests for marketing items to be considered for authorization. In some cases, you will want to submit them to your MLM Expert Attorney for their input prior to granting authorization to use.

Master Intake Process

The Master Intake Process is one of the most important components of the Compliance Management System. This process is used to log all alleged infractions daily. It provides valuable information that will allow you to track each infraction and recall at a glance any of the key areas of importance.

If any issue appears to be alarming, you should bring it to the attention of your supervisor immediately. For example, if you have been given a copy of a flyer a Distributor is going to use in an upcoming appearance on TV and the flyer contains income or product claims, this type of infraction should be brought to the immediate attention of your supervisor so it can be addressed with the Distributor before it appears publicly.

The Master Intake Process can be customized to meet the needs of your company based on any regulatory inquiries from the past.

Using the Master Intake Process allows for the entry of many possible incidents of concern to the department. The first sheet tracks the basics of the case and some of the additional notes and or comments. If a case becomes a large issue, an individual file folder can be set up to keep a running history of your conversations and correspondences.

My preference is to store the logs on Google Sheets. It is easy to pull multiple people into the log and make online updates in real time.
Websites Issues

Track general website infractions, such as prohibited use of the company's logo on a third-party website. Log the infraction and list as much information as possible on a tracking log, including the web address and any names, phone numbers or representative ID numbers on the site. This information will help you locate and contact the Distributor responsible for the infraction.

Once you have determined that an infraction exists and have documented it, begin your investigation, and contact the Distributor about how they will correct it, Alert them of the violation and get a detailed statement from them regarding the issue and the steps they are taking to correct it.

eBay Issues

Track eBay Compliance Infractions; you will need to if your company regulates how and what company products are sold on eBay. eBay offers a program called VERO that assists in taking a product down from the site when necessary — this can be very useful if your company monitors its product sales on eBay. Contact eBay directly about the VERO program and how to apply.

Amazon Activities

Track activities related to Amazon online sales. Amazon is a difficult website to police. Amazon allows people to select a unique (anonymous) name to interact on their webpage. Since people who post do not have to identify themselves, it makes it very difficult to ascertain who is posting. Very similar to what is found on eBay.

There are a couple of ways to open communication with someone who has listed your product for sale on Amazon. Company Compliance staff can initiate an investigation to determine the real name of the person by contacting Amazon. Another way is to purchase your products on Amazon. Use a friend or staff person's contact information. This way you can get a return address, which in some cases will be enough to identify the seller.

To investigate, open the specific post and find the name of the person or entity attempting to sell product on Amazon. Many times, Distributors will identify themselves as your company. That's right, they select your company name as the seller on their listing of your product. This must not be allowed.

When a post looks like it is coming from your company, it makes it very confusing and frustrating for the customers and other Distributors. Prices may vary for similar products listed on Amazon, making it attractive for the general public to purchase on Amazon.

Most companies restrict Distributors from selling their products on Amazon. If someone posts your products and responds that they are not one of your Distributors, there is not much you can do to restrict them from selling your products on Amazon. The only people you can stop from selling on Amazon are your Distributors since they are bound by your Policies and Procedures. Other people, who are not Distributors, will not be bound by your rules.

In order to obtain the identity of the seller, resort to making a purchase of product from the Amazon website. Ask a question of the seller when you pay for the product, "How would I become a Distributor in order to purchase this product in future?"

You will be amazed how many of them will include a flyer or brochure with their name, ID number and website address. In many cases, the fear of loss makes the Distributor share their contact information with the purchaser. The company customer service department may also help identify who the seller is by the contact information they shared!

Policies and Procedures documents usually state that relatives (or friends) may not sell products on behalf of the Distributor to skirt the Policies. This is in direct violation of the Policies and Procedures. This type of behavior must command a short-term suspension so that the Distributor knows the company takes online sales seriously.

If the search for the owner of the listing comes up empty, try communicating with the seller through the Amazon platform.

Facebook Activities

Track activities related to Facebook, obtain the exact link of the Facebook issue, and as much information as possible must be recorded. Screenshots are good for documenting, but you need the exact link to find the post.

Facebook presents high risk for many Direct Selling companies. The biggest exposure is that Distributors go on Facebook and post unauthorized income, drug and weight loss claims. Additionally, Distributors will appear to look like the official company which is confusing to the public and regulators.

Your Compliance Department has the job of monitoring Facebook for unauthorized activities and reaching out to those Distributors to alert them of their potential violations.

When a company establishes their Facebook protocols BEFORE they open their doors, they provide a solid foundation for the Compliance Department to stop offender's right from the beginning.

If a company waits to establish their Facebook protocols until AFTER they open their doors, it becomes very difficult, then, to stop unwanted Facebook posts. It is possible, but it is very difficult.

Facebook issues include the use of the company name and corporate logo without permission. In almost all cases, Direct Selling companies do not allow their Distributors to use their logo or corporate name in the title of a Facebook page. The title or URL for the Facebook page can be monitored and must be changed by the Distributor, when requested by compliance.

Social Media & Use of Your Brand (Logo)

Another important aspect of the Compliance Department is attempting to monitor so many social media websites. With the expansion of the internet and social media, Direct Selling companies may not have addressed social media and the Distributor's ability to participate in it. MLM Expert attorneys are recognizing the need for Policies and Procedures which include social media policies for Distributors.

Social Media represents an exposure for companies to consider further. Companies must secure their URL's, Facebook fan page, their Twitter handle, their YouTube channel, and any other social media names necessary to protect the company brand. If you don't acquire them prior to the company opening, or even before you start any promotions, then your Distributors will grab them.

Many of the concerns of social media center around the use of the company's brand and logo. It is highly recommended that companies develop a separate logo for Distributors to use. The company's main logo must be protected at all costs. The "Independent Distributor" logo allows Distributors to post in social media and easily be identified as an Independent Distributor. Social Media concerns surrounding the brand can also be addressed prior to the company opening its doors.

It is suggested that companies and their lawyers develop a set of Social Media Marketing Guidelines. The base of the guidelines comes from your Policies and Procedures. The rest of the social media guidelines come from the company's preferences for social media behavior. When you work with DSS, we develop a full set of social media marketing guidelines.

Review of Literature, sales aids, and Third-Party Websites

Distributors will submit for approval of self-created websites that promote the company products and opportunity. In many companies, the Distributors are not allowed to create either marketing materials or self-created websites. We strongly recommend not allowing ANY self-created websites right from the formation of the company. If you allow these websites, you put the company at risk. Self-created websites are not easily monitored, and many times include income and product claims that can expose the company from a regulatory standpoint.

Your Compliance Department will receive requests from Distributors for self-recreated literature, marketing materials, and sales aids. Some companies have fun with such requests and have contests allowing Distributors to submit their self-created materials for a company promotion. The Compliance Officer must review such submissions for use of proper distributor logo, graphics, approvals, and medical and drug claims.

Progress Notes

The Progress Notes are used to manually track your progress on one specific case. For example, you would take notes when talking on the phone that is reporting a possible infraction. Use progress notes  whenever a case is going to be escalated to the attorneys. The progress notes will include the person's name, the issue in question, their ID number, their phone number, their email, and their home address. Develop the progress notes as if you are telling a story about the situation.

If possible, putting a date and time on each entry will be beneficial. If needed, escalate the case to the attorney using the precise notes that were taken. Progress notes should include what happened, when it happened, and what was done about it. Keep all progress notes until you have entered them electronically or until the reporting party submits a ticket in writing regarding the potential violation.

Chapter 6

THE SECRET TO COMPLIANCE PROTECTION

COMPLIANCE EDUCATION

When companies get in trouble these days, regulators require compliance training. This chapter will describe the need for compliance training and the many benefits derived from it. Some of the biggest companies in the direct selling industry require compliance training prior to authorizing Distributors to represent their products.

Kevin Grimes is one of the most experienced and accomplished MLM attorneys in America. Over his 23-year career as a network-marketing attorney, he has represented and advised the proverbial "Who's Who" of direct selling and multilevel marketing including Herbalife, Shaklee, Tupperware, USANA, MetaboLife, Mona Vie, and hundreds more.

Contributed by Kevin Grimes, Direct Selling MLM Expert Attorney

Distributor Compliance Virtual Training (VT)

Why you need it!

The FTC established a regulatory guide in 2009 that is still in effect. In a nutshell, it says that MLM companies are liable for the false or unsubstantiated statements of their "endorsers" (or Distributors).

Consider your Compliance training efforts

Is it enough or is it lacking the ability to virtually train and test your Distributors?

To the maximum extent possible, Distributor Compliance Virtual Training is designed to neutralize regulators' complaints and insulate direct selling companies from distributor non-compliance.

Did you know?

- The Federal Trade Commission has specifically stated that marketers (MLM companies) must provide "guidance and training" to the company's distributors in order to avoid potential liability.
- State Attorneys General have started looking to see whether MLM companies are providing distributor compliance training to every single distributor.
- States have started suing MLM companies to put them out of
- business because of the wrongful claims of just one distributor.
- States have started requiring MLM companies to provide every single distributor compliance training and testing to ensure that distributors understand what they have learned.
- States have started prohibiting MLM companies from: (1) allowing distributors to enroll customers or other distributors; or (2) paying their distributors, unless and until each distributor has received adequate compliance training and passed a compliance test.
- MLM Companies are liable for the false or unsubstantiated statements of their distributors.

The FTC has stated marketers (MLM companies) must provide

"guidance and training" to their distributors regarding legal and regulatory compliance. Without such guidance and training, a company's potential liability is unlimited.

Regulators are beginning to expect and demand that MLM companies provide guidance, training, education, and testing to all their distributors regarding all applicable aspects of legal and regulatory compliance on a continuing basis.

From outside and inside of the MLM industry, the distributor compliance "bar" is being raised. Companies that fail to raise their distributor compliance educational standards will leave themselves susceptible to regulatory attack.

Just as the days of merely "reactive" compliance efforts are long gone (because regulators and courts require companies to be "proactive"), the days of no or minimal compliance training, testing, and accountability will soon become extinct. The distributor compliance program Herbalife got crammed down its throat by the FTC is a good example.

The training that one Attorney General wanted to see had nothing to do with distributor recruiting. It had nothing to do with personal development. It had nothing to do with leadership training. It had nothing to do with the business building. It had everything to do with legal and regulatory compliance education, testing, tracking, and accountability.

Like the "training and guidance" the Federal Trade Commission wants to see, it has everything to do with legal and regulatory compliance. Attorneys General want to see what the company is doing to guide, train, education and test its distributors on a continuing basis relative to "consumer protection compliance standards" . . . which is to say all applicable areas of consumer protection law.

History teaches the MLM industry that there are the seven elements to a world-class compliance operation:

    1. A rock-solid legal/contractual foundation with the company's

distributors [i.e., the Distributor Agreement and Policies and Procedures];

2. Comprehensive compliance education and testing for distributors on the topics that have resulted in regulatory enforcement actions and civil lawsuits;

3. Properly trained and effective corporate compliance personnel;

4. Thorough Standard Operative Procedures ("SOPs") that address all potential compliance issues;

5. Proactive monitoring of distributor activities [e.g. regular web surfing "Secret Shoppers," at meetings and trainings, etc.];

6. Effective correction of non-compliant activities; and

7. Documentation/record keeping of the company's compliance efforts.

Most direct sellers have six of the seven pieces in place. However, the one that is universally lacking is Number 2 -- comprehensive compliance education for distributors on the topics that have resulted in regulatory enforcement actions and civil lawsuits.

MLM Compliance VT was born out of what Kevin saw as a significant and dangerous void in the universe of direct selling distributor compliance. Direct selling distributor compliance education is a massive need that simply is not being met.

To the maximum extent possible, MLM Compliance VT is designed to neutralize regulators' complaints and insulate direct selling companies from distributor non-compliance. It is a system that incorporates all of the features enumerated in the Viridian and North American Power cases, but with vastly more robust content.

In order for an MLM company to limit (or eliminate) its potential liability -- someone, whether it is the company or a third party, must provide "guidance and training" to the company's "agents" (distributors).

MLM Compliance VT Includes:

Compliance training includes a selection from the modules that have already been recorded. We will customize your training by including one of your team on the videos. In fact, we can upload up to 30 additional minutes of your customized content.

Wouldn't it be well received to have your founder or owner do the introduction to the virtual Compliance Training system. It will allow your company to see your leader endorsing your NEW MLM Compliance Virtual Training.

MLM Compliance VT Do's and Don'ts Edition – Is designed for new distributors and presents the content so that they are not overwhelmed with legal and regulatory information. The Do's and Don'ts can be customized for each company. The owner/founder is invited to come to the studio and tape an opening and a few blips to introduce Kevin and the training upcoming.

As the name suggests, the Do's and Don'ts Edition presents distributors with very simple and concrete direction relative to their new businesses. The total run time is 45 minutes (less if one or modules are omitted), and it has a total testing pool of over 100 randomized questions, of which the viewer will be presented roughly 50. Based on the Modules selected, the number of questions will be adjusted. The subjects covered in MLM Compliance VT include:

- Introduction ñ to include your owner/founder
- Pyramids
- Income Claims
- Securities
- Franchises and Business Opportunities
- Lotteries
- Buying Clubs
- Certificate Programs
- Auto-ships and Auto-orders
- Cooling off laws

As you can see MLM Compliance VT, will meet all your Compliance needs and can be customized to your company's culture. This unique training will also give you reassurance that your team has been trained with regulatory considerations in place. MLM Compliance VT provides a layer of protection in order to isolate the company from wrong doing distributors.

Every CEO and corporate compliance department has had to deal with the rogue distributor who believes they can do or say anything they want in the building of their businesses. MLM Compliance VT can address potential distributor issues before they put the company at risk.

Let's look at a few recent developments and some "changing realties" regarding the MLM industry with you.

The Federal Trade Commission

First, the Federal Trade Commission promulgated its Guides Concerning the Use of Endorsements and Testimonials in Advertising (Title 16 of the Code of Federal Regulations, Part 255), which became effective on December 1, 2009. The Guides tell us where the FTC's "head" is relative to the topic of endorsements and testimonials of third parties (agents), like Distributors, and their principals (MLM companies).

Title 16 Code of Federal Regulations Part 255 ß 255.1 General considerations.

Advertisers are subject to liability for false or unsubstantiated statements made through endorsements, or for failing to disclose material connections between themselves and their endorsers [see ß 255.5]. Endorsers also may be liable for statements made in the course of their endorsements.

The sentence above means that MLM companies are liable for the false or unsubstantiated statements of their "endorsers," that is to say, its Distributors. I realize that is probably not "news" to you.

However, it is interesting to note that in its Examples to Section 255.1(d), the FTC stated the following regarding "guidance and training."

Example 5: A skin care products advertiser participates in a blog advertising service. The service matches up advertisers with bloggers who will promote the advertiser's products on their personal blogs. The advertiser requests that a blogger try a new body lotion and write a review of the product on her blog. Although the advertiser does not make any specific claims about the lotion's ability to cure skin conditions and the blogger does not ask the advertiser whether there is substantiation for the claim, in her review the blogger writes that the lotion cures eczema and recommends the product to her blog readers who suffer from this condition. The advertiser is subject to liability for misleading or unsubstantiated representations made through the blogger's endorsement. The blogger also is subject to liability for misleading or unsubstantiated representations made in the course of her endorsement. The blogger is also liable if she fails to disclose clearly and conspicuously that she is being paid for her services. [See ß 255.5.]

In order to limit its potential liability, the advertiser should ensure that the advertising service provides guidance and training to its bloggers concerning the need to ensure that statements they make are truthful and substantiated. The advertiser should also monitor bloggers who are being paid to promote its products and take steps necessary to halt the continued publication of deceptive representations when they are discovered.

The bottom line is -- in order for an MLM company to limit (or eliminate) its potential liability -- someone, whether it is the company or a third party, must provide "guidance and training" to the company's "agents" (Distributors). Virtually NO MLM companies are doing this.

Changing Reality Number 1 -- MLM companies must provide "guidance and training" to their Distributors regarding legal and regulatory compliance. Without such guidance and training, a company's potential liability is unlimited. Below are examples demonstrating what regulators were expecting, and demand relative to MLM distributor compliance training.

Letter from the New Jersey Attorney General

CHRIS CHRISTIE
Governor

KIM GUADAGNO
Lt. Governor

New Jersey Office of the Attorney General
Division of Consumer Affairs
Office of Consumer Protection
124 Halsey Street, 7ᵗʰ Floor, Newark, NJ 07102

PAULA T. DOW
Attorney General

THOMAS R. CALCAGNI
Director

July 26, 2011

RECEIVED
JUL 28 2011
BY

Mailing Address:
P.O. Box 45025
Newark, NJ 07101
(973) 504-6200

Re:

Dear

It was a pleasure meeting with you,   and   on July 20, 2011 to discuss   proposed network marketing by independent sales agents of its   product. While network marketing has its "dark side," I am encouraged that your client was receptive to meeting with the New Jersey Division of Consumer Affairs to discuss the proposed marketing plan. As a follow up to that meeting, I am writing to request that   provide the Division with the following materials for its review:

1. All materials used by   to recruit its independent sales agents.
2. All materials used by   to select its independent sales agents.
3. All materials used by   to train its independent sales agents.
4. All materials used by   to test its independent sales agents.
5. All materials used by   to retain or engage persons to act as its independent sales agents.
6. All materials used by   to compensate its independent sales agents.
7. All materials used by   to provide continuing consumer protection compliance standards/guidelines and education to its independent sales agents.
8. All materials showing an organizational or flow chart related to the network marketing of   product by its independent sales agents.
9. All materials used by   as a compliance and management protocol/guidelines for network marketing by independent sales agents of its   product.
10. All materials relating to   Compliance Committee.
11. All materials relating to   Customer Service Department.
12.   "Welcome Kit" containing all support materials provided to independent sales agents.

Please arrange to have these materials provided to the Division (you may have the materials mailed or delivered to me) by August 10, 2011. If more time is needed, please let me know. Once these materials are received and reviewed, I would like to meet again and discuss the Division's analysis and any concerns that it might have regarding your client's marketing program.

Very truly yours,

Cindy K. Miller, Deputy Director

cc -   Jennifer Micco, Supervising Investigator - OCP

New Jersey Is An Equal Opportunity Employer • Printed on Recycled Paper and Recyclable

The first document is a letter one of Kevin's clients received from the New Jersey Attorney General's Office. It is important to note that the company was not in trouble. It was not being investigated. The New

Jersey Attorney General simply wanted to know more about the company. The letter specifically requested information, documents, and resources in 12 areas. Four were particularly illuminating. The Attorney General's office wanted to see:

- All materials used to train the company's independent sales agents;
- All materials used to test the company's independent sales agents;
- All materials used to provide continuing consumer protection compliance standards /guidelines and education to the company's independent sales agents; and iv.
- All materials used as a compliance and management protocol/guidelines for network marketing by the company's independent sales agents.

The training the Attorney General wanted to see had nothing to do with distributor recruiting. It had nothing to do with personal development. It had nothing to do with leadership training. It had nothing to do with the business building. It had everything to do with legal and regulatory compliance education, testing, tracking, and accountability.

Like the "training and guidance" the Federal Trade Commission wants to see, it has everything to do with legal and regulatory compliance. The Attorney General wants to see what the company is doing to guide, train, educate and test its Distributors on a continuing basis relative to "consumer protection compliance standards" . . . which is to say all applicable areas of consumer protection law.

Changing Reality Number 2 - Regulators are beginning to expect and demand that MLM companies provide guidance, training, education, and testing to all their Distributors regarding all applicable aspects of legal and regulatory compliance on a continuing basis.

The Viridian and North American Power Cases

The Maryland Public Service Commission ("PSC") sued two electricity MLMs, Viridian Energy and North American Power ("NAP"), to revoke their licenses to offer electricity. That is to say, Maryland was trying to completely shut down these two companies from operating in Maryland. The PCS alleged that the Distributors of both companies had engaged in deceptive practices.

Maryland v. Viridian

In the Viridian case, the lawsuit was precipitated merely by one flyer and one classified advertisement! These two pieces resulted in the allegation that "Viridian uses misleading, and deceptive practices..."

That's all it took to start the lawsuit.

Prior to the lawsuit, Viridian provided to its Distributors a comprehensive set of Policies and Procedures and a one-page document entitled Marketing Don'ts. Both documents addressed issues such as: misleading or deceptive advertising; income claims; savings claims; and other typical consumer protection law issues.

The PCS's position was – That is not nearly enough distributor compliance training. It's not even close.

In order to settle the case, Viridian agreed to develop Viridian University. (All text below is verbatim from the Joint Recommendation of the Staff of the Public Service Commission of Maryland and Viridian Energy.) As described in the Joint Recommendation of the Staff of the Public Service Commission of Maryland and Viridian Energy, Viridian University is an online training portal for Viridian Distributors.

Phase 1 – The first phase of the Viridian University launch included 45 minutes in 13 modules regarding compliance training, testing, and certification covering topics such as "Why Compliance?" "Internal Compliance Procedures", and "Proper Customer Enrollment." For the initial launch, all current and future Viridian

Distributors will be required to complete Phase 1 prior to being eligible to earn commissions on their sales.

Phase 2 - Phase 2 of the Viridian University launch will include market-specific training. Similar to the Phase 1 launch, all current and future Viridian Distributors will be required to complete this prior to being eligible to earn commissions on their Viridian sales. Viridian envisions that the market-specific training will be required prior to customer enrollment in the future; however, a release date for this functionality has not yet been set.

Phase 3 - The final phase of the Viridian University launch will include ongoing continuing education for associates (new products, new markets, regulatory changes, etc.). Similar to the Phases 1 and 2, all current and future Viridian Distributors will be required to complete these training modules, as new information is available.

Page 10 of the Joint Recommendation of the Staff of the Public Service Commission of Maryland and Viridian Energy provided:

> *All current and future Viridian Distributors will be required to complete each training phase and pass a randomly generated test. In the initial implementation of this new system, Viridian will not pay commissions to its Viridian Distributors until the Independent Associate passes the test. Upon completion of the necessary technological enhancements, the Independent Associate will not be able to enroll customers with Viridian until he or she has passed the test. Once an Independent Associate has passed the test for all required modules, the Associate will have passed Compliance Certification and be eligible to receive commissions.*

Maryland v. North American Power

The facts in North American Power (NAP) case were similar to those in the Viridian case. It is interesting to note that like the Viridian case, it took very little to energize the PSC to file its complaint. As you will note from paragraphs 5 and 6 of the Complaint, the PSC Staff alleged that only one representative made misrepresentations to a consumer! That's all it took, misrepresentations by one rep to one prospective customer.

It is also worth noting that NAP also required its representatives to undertake approximately 1-1½ hours of live compliance training by NAP's area managers.

In the eyes of the State of Maryland, even one and a half hours of live compliance training was not sufficient. Like Viridian, in order to retain its License NAP was required to develop an online compliance education training and testing program that its representatives are required to pass annually. Maryland required the NAP program to cover more regulatory compliance topics than Viridian's! NAP was required to pay the State of Maryland a civil penalty of $100,000 (. . . and if you multiply that number by 49 states . . .)

I anticipate that regulators will soon establish this approach as the "best practices" of distributor compliance education and expect all MLM companies to do so.

Changing Reality Number 3 -- From outside and inside of the MLM industry, the distributor compliance "bar" is being raised. Companies that fail to raise their distributor compliance educational standards will leave themselves susceptible to regulatory attack.

Fourth, I would be remiss in my responsibilities as an MLM attorney if I did not bring to companies' attention the fact that every MLM Company's distributor compliance education program is either non-existent or woefully inadequate relative to what regulators are expecting today and in the future.

Changing Reality Number 4 -- Just as the days of merely "reactive" compliance efforts are long gone (because regulators and courts require companies to be "proactive"), the days of no or minimal compliance training, testing, and accountability will soon become extinct.

Perhaps the most telling indication of regulatory expectations is found in the Remediation Plan of Viridian Energy. Part 4 (2)(d) thereof provides:

> *Goals of the Training Modifications and Improvements: Recent compliance challenges have underscored the importance to Viridian that its Viridian Distributors are properly trained and have sufficiently absorbed the training materials. Viridian's training modifications have been designed to ensure, to the greatest extent possible, that the Viridian Distributors understand . . . [compliance]*
>
> *... To accomplish these goals, Viridian has begun implementation of an online training system, complete with testing/certifications, so that Viridian can ensure that all of the training material is being conveyed and understood. By requiring that Associates complete a test along with their online training, Viridian is ensuring that Associates have not only read the training documents and watched the videos, but that they understand and retain the concepts therein so that they can market on behalf of Viridian in a compliant manner.*

We're not talking about things regulators were doing 10 or 15 years ago. We're talking about things they are doing now. All of these things I just mentioned happened in 2011. These cases make clear that "testing," specifically "randomized testing," has rocketed to the forefront of regulators' expectations regarding distributor compliance.

Kevin Grimes has developed an online direct selling compliance training, testing, tracking, and accountability program that might dovetail with what you are doing relative to distributor compliance. It is called *MLM Compliance VT*, and can be found at www.mlmcompliancevt.com. It is not a concept -- it is live and fully operational. Since it launched, over 200,000 Distributors have been trained, tested, and certified.

MLM Compliance VT was born out of what I see as a significant and dangerous void in the industry of direct selling distributor compliance. Direct selling distributor compliance education is a massive need that simply is not being met.

To the maximum extent possible, MLM Compliance VT is designed to neutralize regulators' complaints and insulate direct selling companies from distributor non-compliance. It is a system that incorporates all of the features enumerated in the Viridian and North American Power cases, but with vastly more robust content. It offers three different levels of courses:

1. *MLM Compliance VT Leadership Mastery Edition*
The Leadership Mastery Edition is a thermo-nuclear, scorched earth, mother-of-all-distributor compliance education resource. It is designed for corporate compliance personnel, high-level Distributors, Distributors who have significant public exposure, and Distributors who develop their own marketing or training materials. The Leadership Mastery Edition has roughly five and a half hours of video training (broken into 4 to 10-minute segments) on nine different regulatory "hot topics" that have generated regulatory enforcement actions against MLM companies. Each topic is a "course," and at the end of each course, the viewer is presented with a comprehensive list of "Do's and Don'ts" relative to the operation of an MLM Distributorship. The Leadership Mastery Edition has a total testing pool of over 400 randomized questions, of which the viewer will be presented roughly 200.

2. *MLM Compliance VT: The Professional Compliance Edition*
The Professional Edition is approximately two and half- hours of video training. It is designed for mid-level Distributors and leaders who are "up and coming" business-builders. The Professional Compliance Edition contains all of the "bottom line" information of the Leadership Mastery Edition. However, it does not include the extensive discussions of case law and comprehensive analysis of statutory definitions that the Leadership Mastery Edition includes. It has a total testing pool of

over 250 randomized questions, of which the viewer will be presented roughly 125.

HIGHLY RECOMMENDED FOR DISTRIBUTORS
3. *MLM Compliance VT Do's and Don'ts Edition*
The Do's and Don'ts Edition is approximately 45 minutes of video training. It is designed for new Distributors and presents the content so that they are not overwhelmed with legal and regulatory information. As the name suggests, the Do's and Don'ts Edition presents Distributors with very simple and concrete direction relative to their new businesses. It has a total testing pool of over 100 randomized questions, of which the viewer will be presented roughly 50.

The Bottom Line

Reality #1 = An MLM Company's single biggest regulatory risk is distributor compliance.

Reality # 2 - An MLM Company's single biggest area of exposure within distributor compliance is its complete lack of any regulatory compliance training, testing, tracking, and accountability.

Reality # 3 - Since the inception of this industry, even the largest direct selling companies in the world have been completely unable to develop adequate compliance training programs.
So . . . what are you going to do?

Chapter 7

COMMUNICATION PROTOCOLS
TESTIMONIALS, EVENTS AND CONFERENCE CALLS

In the direct selling industry there are three valuable marketing communication tools, testimonials, events and up-line conference calls. They are used to generate attention and sales and valuable strategies, but they also can be a compliance nightmare if not managed and monitored.

Testimonials

The most common tool is the testimonial – where someone attests to the effectiveness or quality of the product. We've all heard them because a *POWERFUL TESTIMONIAL* leads to product sales. Nothing is more powerful than a testimonial about being a user of the product. What type of testimonial will it be - A compliant one.

It is important to have testimonials developed by Distributors and then reviewed by the Compliance Department. This process is time-consuming, but it will pay off greatly if in the future the company comes under regulatory inquiry. Distributors should be taught in a specifically organized manner how to create and deliver compliant testimonials. Testimonials should be based on their own personal experience with the product and many companies do not allow third party testimonials, especially if it is a health and wellness company. Third party testimonials include sharing your best friend's or your spouse's testimonial. Testimonials are so important therefore CMS provides a testimonial worksheet to assist with composing a compliant testimonial.

Testimonial Worksheet

The Testimonial Worksheet provides guidelines for Distributors to create a compliant testimonial. The form can be presented to distributors via a conference call or in-person training. We have seen Distributors work with their sponsor over the phone in order to complete the form. It is recommended that the company have a couple different forms for Distributors to choose from when customizing a testimonial.

A testimonial can be about products or the business opportunity and can be a written document or delivered personally. Therefore it is wise to teach Distributors to create different types of testimonials. The best testimonials are short and to the point. If a distributor attempts to deliver a product, an opportunity, or company testimonial all at the same time the testimonial becomes too long and loses its impact.

There are four parts to a testimonial.
1. Share your name, professional or personal background, as well as where you are from.
2. Share how you were introduced to the company or product.
3. Share your experience with the product; state the facts and the results what is the challenge? How is it different now?
4. Finally, keep it positive with no medical or income claims. Additionally, do not discuss former companies or the results with other company's products.

Example: I am Stephanie from Clearwater, Florida and I am a 4th grade teacher. My best friend told me about this incredible product that I just had to try. I had difficulties sleeping. For whatever reason,

I could not sleep 6 hours straight which led to me being grouchy and miserable at my job. Then I started taking the product and within a few nights I was sleeping like a baby and felt more energized and refreshed in the mornings.

Here is a simple worksheet to create a compliant testimonial like the one above.

COMPANY LOGO

Testimonial Worksheet
We would like to hear from YOU!

This worksheet is for you to develop your _____ testimonial. Please indicate your comments clearly and be sure to complete the bottom including your phone number, in case we would like to contact you for additional information. Thank you for agreeing to share your story with others – together we can make a difference!

My Name is_____, my personal and/or professional background is:
My name is Donna Marie and I am a teacher.

How I was introduced to our Company:
The first time I saw this product was at my exercise class from my neighbor.

My experience with our product (or services) is:

- State Facts:
  I have had trouble doing my normal exercises in the water, my flexibility to limited.

- State Results:
  Ever since I have been taking (PRODUCT), I have had excellent workouts. I move flexibly and without the normal aches that I used to.

Keep it POSITIVE!

No income or product claims or names of former companies will be allowed or accepted in testimonials.

I hereby give (Company) _____ permission to publish my comments in part or in full.

_____   _____
Authorizing Signature   Id #

_____   _____
Print First Name   Print Last Name

_____   _____
Daytime Phone   Date

Please email to:

Testimonials must be reviewed in writing, prior to use at ANY posting, official company event, opportunity meeting or training event. Distributors should sign the testimonial worksheet before sending it to the Compliance Department for review.

Once distributors have developed a testimonial it is important to become comfortable with it. Practice with their sponsor or fellow Distributors so that it becomes second nature. It is valuable to request the Testimonial Release form to be executed at the same time you gather the testimonial worksheet.

Testimonial Release Form

The Testimonial Release form is comparable to or could be a media release as noted below. It grants permission to the company to use a Distributor's testimonial in any media, such as video or print.

COMPANY BRAND LOGO

MEDIA RELEASE FORM

I, _____ DBA _____

grant permission to (the **COMPANY LEGAL NAME**), hereafter referred to as the "Company", its agents, employees, or representative the irrevocable and unrestricted right to reproduce testimonials, photographs and/or video images for the purpose of publication, promotion, illustration, advertising, or trade, in any manner or in any medium. I hereby release the Company and its legal representatives for all claims and liability relating to said reproductions and furthermore, I grant permission to use my statements that were given during an interview, presentation or guest appearance, with or without my name, for the purpose of advertising and publicity without restriction. I waive my right to any compensation for use in publications and promotions including:

Broadcasts, Videos, Email, Recruiting Brochures, Training, Summits, Conferences, Newsletters, Magazines, General Publications, Websites or Social Media.

I acknowledge that I am: [   ] over the age of 18
                           [   ] the legal guardian of the following

Please **initial** the paragraph below.

[   ] I understand and acknowledge that I am not receiving any compensation now or in the future, and hereby waive any right to inspect or approve the finished photographs or electronic matter that may be used in conjunction with them now or in the future, whether that use is known to me or unknown, and I waive any right to royalties or other compensation arising from or related to the use of the image.

I understand that I am free to address any specific questions regarding this release by submitting those questions in writing prior to signing, and I agree that my failure to do so will be interpreted as a free and knowledgeable acceptance of the terms of this release.

PLEASE PRINT
Name/Company: _____ Date: ___/___/___

Mailing Address: _____
                  STREET   CITY/STATE/ZIP

Email: _____ Phone: _____

Authorized Representative Signature: _____
If Legal guardian, please print your name: _____

Office use only

Broadcast/event: _____ Recording/event date: _____

This form is necessary for all parties involved and allows the company to use the testimonial for advertising or on any of its publications without the fear of retribution. The person doing the testimonial signs the form, unless the testimonial is by a minor (which is rare) in which case a parent or guardian must sign the release form on the minor's behalf.

The testimonial release form is a simple one-page document that authorizes the company to use a Distributors testimonial including their name, voice, photograph and likeness. It also includes consent to be included in photographs and video production. This is the release that should be used for the general distributor population and if the occasion arises customers of the products if they are making testimonials.

Additional Communication Requests

It is smart to keep the lines of communication open between the Compliance Department and field, especially field leaders. Any information that can be obtained and documented regarding Distributor field activities is important for reporting Compliance efforts.

The CMS encourages Distributors report any advertising and/or marketing efforts on an Advertising Request Form. This information may be gathered online or by way of scanned documents sent or submitted to the Compliance Department.

Advertising Request Form

An Advertising Request form allows distributors to submit a request to use their own advertising materials to market their business. If your company does not permit Distributors to develop and use their own advertising materials, this form will still be necessary.

If this form is to be used, it is possible for the IT department to place the form online for electronic submission. It is important for

Distributors to communicate their advertising ideas, marketing materials, and any type of advertisements to compliance for prior approval. Even if your Policies and Procedures state that Distributors may not advertise or create their own marketing materials, they will do it. In the long run it is better to ask what they are doing than discover it later.

Event Registration Protocol

Events refer to opportunity meetings and represent high Compliance risk and you must know what is going on in the field. An event registration form is to be used by any distributor requesting authorization to participate in an event to promote your products and/or opportunity. If handled improperly events can be a RED FLAG to regulatory authorities. The company may use an event registration form to review all event requests. Then the company gives authorization, and performs random monitoring to make sure the Distributors comply with the event S.O.P.s.

All requests must be completed in writing and submitted to Compliance prior to the event. Distributors must complete an event request form when a business opportunity meeting has over 50 participants, or to receive authorization to participate in any type of vendor event. The form must be used whenever products are being offered for sale. Distributors may include any assistance they are asking for the company to give. The distributor must describe what they want to do at the event and if they are going to be selling or offering samples of any product. The form is to be used as an acknowledgment that the distributor has read and understand the advertising and promotional materials section of your company's Policies and Procedures. Distributors who do not register events will be considered in violation of the company Policies & Procedures and maybe open to sanctions.

Event Registration Log

Once the office receives the Event Request, it is to be logged on the

Master Event Registration Log. This log is to be placed on Google Sheets, so it is available online to everyone on staff. It needs to be available to everyone on staff so different levels of management can look and see what Distributors are having events.

Have your Compliance Officer log all event requests, even ones that have been turned down. The Company has a responsibility to track all information regarding events. When you have every item written in one log then you have a chronological log of what was and was not approved. If any problems occur, you will have a log showing your company did or did not approve the event as well as exactly what was approved. The registration log is necessary to collect information on all event requests.

Distributors Acknowledgment for Hosting a Public Presentation

Distributors must execute the Acknowledgment for hosting a public presentation (for more than 50 people) prior to producing a public event. All Distributor speakers must also sign off on the document.

Distributors must be authorized to present at public events, opportunity meetings, trainings and/or company-sponsored events including Annual Events and Retreats. Regulators attend public presentations of Direct Selling companies. Don't think for a minute that they don't. They even bring recording devices in and create unauthorized video evidence. Registration at large company events such as regional or annual events can be tightened up by requiring an ID such as a Driver's License to register.

It may even be necessary for a company to hire security for large events. You want to avoid unexpected surprises that may happen at a large event. You just NEVER know what will happen at your event!

I attended a direct selling company's annual event and there was a very large Greek wedding reception in the next hotel ballroom. The direct selling company's booking representative must not have asked what other events would be held in the next room during their convention when she made the hotel arrangements. The reception got progressively louder and louder. When the toasts started with lusty cheers of "Opa!" it was so loud you couldn't hear what was happening in our meeting room.

The planner for the direct selling event was notified repeatedly to request the people at the reception keep the noise level down (if possible).

Well, the wedding party announced to the entire reception we made a request for them to calm down. We heard every word. After, it was so loud, several of the men from our meeting went out into the hallway to see if they could ask them to quiet down.

There was then a loud ruckus out in the hallway. Someone threw a punch and a man fell into the meeting room of the direct selling company. It looked like it was going be a gang war clash between the two groups.

There was no security present at the direct selling event. Someone with a level head from both groups broke up the skirmish. Both groups were embarrassed into finally calming down and going back to their conference room and wedding reception. Talk about an unexpected interruption at both events!

Keeping Track of Conference Calls

The Conference Call Review Form should be used to review Distributor conference calls. It provides the necessary items required to monitor a conference call. When monitoring a call, get as much detail as possible especially the name of the host of the call. Be sure to note any dialogue that  may be questionable regarding compliance with company policies or that could raise the interest of a regulator.

Conference call attendees often talk over one another, making it difficult for you to hear the speaker. In the event, you cannot determine who is speaking, make a note of who spoke just after that person. You may also contact the host after the call to determine who was on the call. In many cases conference calls are recorded.

If you note any infractions, contact the Distributor(s) who committed the infraction and alert them. If the infraction is questionable, you may call the person and explain how to improve for the next call. If an actual infraction occurred, a letter or email may be necessary. Regardless, it is recommended that you document it on the Master Intake Log.

Video Checklist

It is smart for new companies to secure their company YouTube channel. Make it an official resource for company-developed and/or authorized videos. Require Distributors to send in any self-created videos to Compliance for prior written authorization.

It is almost impossible to pull non-compliant videos from YouTube. Monitoring and requiring pre-approval before posting are essential. When you do find a noncompliant video, you must take action. Post it on the Master Intake log and note any attempts to get it removed or notify the owner to take it down.

If you have not been able to determine who the Distributor is and the video is still up, you can put a small sentence under the comments section stating that this video is not authorized from X Company. Be sure to note your repeated attempts to address this with the video owner.

Company Convention Compliance Audit - Required

Prior to the event, the Compliance Department must review a complete list of all Distributors being recognized at the event. It is not wise to recognize a distributor with outstanding compliance issues.

A Compliance Department staff person should attend and perform a convention audit at each major company event or convention. Compliance, even if not speaking, must be visible at company sponsored events and trainings. This shows the field that the company is serious about compliance. It presents very well. If the company plays by the rules and is concerned about providing compliance  education at the event, it must be documented by the compliance staff.

The Compliance Officer should have some involvement in the planning process for all company events. The Officer will be responsible for taking notes at the meetings pertaining to any compliance issues seen.

The actual meeting should also be documented, briefly and in writing. For example, the total number of attendees, the location, the dates, what was covered about compliance at the event.

Many times, owners, founders, or general managers don't see the importance of having Compliance at such events. What we have found is that Distributors are very appreciative to have a visible Compliance Department. It confirms the company's resolve to have all Distributors informed and are encouraged to remain compliant.

In the Compliance Management System, it is recommended to have at least a 20 - 30-minute presentation on compliance at every regional (road shows, 10 city tours, etc.) and annual event. Most Distributors react extremely positively when hearing from compliance. They feel more secure and aware of the efforts the company has taken to "play by the rules." Compliance is a powerful and positive resource that must be utilized and visible during the planning and implementation of company-sponsored events.

Use the following Compliance Audit Protocols when setting event dates and confirming that compliance is available to perform these protocols.

Company Convention Audit Protocols

At any leadership event, regional event, quarterly and annual event, the Compliance Officer will be responsible for ensuring that the event compliance protocol be followed.

Prior To Event

Secure release forms for speakers and testimonial participants. Use the Speaker/Testimonial Release Form found in the Compliance Management System (CMS).

Owners and/or founders must have a brief Compliance meeting, no less than twenty minutes in duration, with the Compliance Officer. The Compliance Officer will file any progress notes, any Compliance consultant check lists or handouts, the meeting agenda, as well as Speaker/Testimonial Release Forms.

During Event

It would be suggested that participants verify their identity at registration by presenting a driver's license or state I.D. There is usually a business opportunity meeting before the official meeting kicks off. It is the Compliance Officer's responsibility to audit the meeting for noncompliance activity and document any issues or concerns.

It is necessary for the Compliance Officer to be at the meeting to audit and document the event. Progress notes must be kept with compliance activities noted.

If the compliance consultant or company's Expert Attorney is presenting at the general meeting, the Compliance Officer should be present and involved in any planning kick off meetings, presentations and wrap up meeting.

Company must display income and health disclaimers in appropriate areas. Always place disclaimers in places where income and health claims are being made such as at business opportunity meetings, and product testimonials.

After Event

There are usually key leadership meetings, immediately after the annual or regional events. The Compliance Officer should be included in those meetings as well.

Chapter 8
COMPLIANCE PREPAREDNESS

COMPLIANCE TRAINING on How to Build a Business for Distributors

We have already discussed the need or compliance training. You must have a process for tracking compliance training. It is a running log of all compliance-focused training. Many companies now require Distributors to complete compliance specific training in order to be certified to be an active Distributor.

Additional training has become a key part of Compliance and it is the Compliance Officer's job to track training that has been completed.

It is beneficial to track who goes through Compliance training at corporate events. Keeping these metrics is important, if and when needing them in case of a regulatory investigation.
Trainings must be structured to teach:

- How to deliver an acceptable, compliant testimonial. Product education
- How to run an opportunity meeting
- How to run a regional company-sponsored event
- How to share the opportunity in a compliant manner How

to sign up a new customer
- How to run a conference call
- How to sign up a new Distributor

Another key component involved in the compliance of any company is related to the amount of compliance education that is done in the field. The level of compliance training will initially be a decision made by the company. Compliance training must include education that Distributors must avoid making income claims or product claims while presenting the company products or opportunity.

Compliance training also includes providing marketing guidelines addressing key areas of concern for Distributors. Distributors want and need specific guidelines to follow in order to maintain their good standing with the company.

The expense for compliance training can vary. There are virtual training options that are currently available for training. Virtual training is highly recommended. It allows the participants to be tested and have their answers recorded. If the Distributor makes a mistake, the system will not allow them to continue until they review and revise their answer.

Regulators today, are expecting companies to provide comprehensive compliance training. We have seen what is required of North American Power and Viridian regarding compliance training. It was not an option; it was a requirement. Therefore, I highly recommend MLM compliance VT (see chapter 6 for more detail.)

Ongoing compliance training is one of the key components to keep the company free of excessive regulatory scrutiny.

There are numerous types of compliance training available in the industry today provided by only a handful of resources. The company may decide to produce their own training, they may choose to have an outside consultant help in the development of the training or they may even consider contracting for the intense training that some of the MLM Expert attorneys provide.

In the event of a regulatory action against the company, the outcome could be that the regulators will require some additional Distributor training. The training may educate the Distributors on product and income claim red flags, as well as the fact that the company sells products to customers and does not pay a commission for the recruitment of other Distributors.

Compliance Preparedness

The following information should be shared with staff and could be reformatted as standalone document.

In the unlikely event that our company comes under investigation; you should be prepared for the unexpected. Actions we take, or don't take, in the early hours of a government investigation can have costly consequences for any company. At the root of this is the importance of having a plan.

There are different types of governmental investigations:
- a subpoena, a phone call,
- search warrant of the premises or
- an on-site request to interview employees.

If regulators come "knocking" with a search warrant this is obviously the most stressful type of government contact because it is unexpected and they take employees by surprise, which naturally puts people on edge.

The subpoena-initiated investigation usually occurs in this manner:

- A subpoena is given to the receptionist (or whomever is at the desk), which gives the agents the right to search the premises and to take certain information from the company without the company's consent.

- Employees are rounded up by the agents conducting the search and sequestered to a certain area while the search is in progress. Attempts will be made to interview the staff. Removal of all company related items might be taken. This includes, but is not limited to, computers (laptop and desktop), cameras, videos, any and all files, business cell phones and personal cell phones IF you retrieve your business email on your personal cell, furniture, compliance records, HR records, and bank related items.
- Staff may be searched. Be aware that anything you have on you may be seized (i.e., knives, guns, drugs, or drug paraphernalia). If you take prescriptions, be sure they are in the appropriate container with your name and doctor's information clearly listed.
- Personal items may also be seized, so please do not bring in anything into the office that is irreplaceable.

Naturally, this can be very intimidating, and an unprepared employee may feel panicky or helpless. Therefore, it is so important that you are all trained on what to do and what your rights are when dealing with the regulators.

First and foremost, you have the right to decline requests to be interviewed and that is the directive of the company. Refrain from conversations with the agents. If questioning you is part of the investigation, always remember that you do have the right to have an attorney present during any questioning.

The Compliance Officer will obtain a copy of the warrant for review to begin to determine its scope and locations to be searched. The Compliance Officer will also identify the lead investigator and note all government agencies and personnel involved. Communication is critical to understanding the scope of the investigation and to establish a working rapport with the regulators, if at all possible.

Key points to keep in mind:

- This is extremely important to REMAIN CALM. The Designated point person of contact is the Compliance Officer. Immediate notification of the warrant and the governmental presence is imperative. Do NOT answer any questions in the interim. The Compliance Officer will promptly make a call to outside counsel. The Compliance Officer will also advise the COO and company owners of the situation. If the Compliance Officer is not available, immediately contact the COO.

- Preserve documents. Do not hide anything or have the appearance of doing so. Depending on the scope of the search warrant, purses may be part of a search. Please do not attempt to place items in your purse during the search. If purses are not part of the warrant, you do not want to draw attention to yourself or any suspicious looking activity.

- If you are on the phone during an investigation, CALMLY end the call without providing the caller with any information. Do not accidentally draw attention to yourself or the situation.

- During an investigation, do not text or make any calls from your phone. If you are caught, your phone may be seized.

- We would prefer you decline the request for interviews; however, if questioned, your responses should be truthful. Upon release by the agents, go home and do not discuss the situation with anyone by communicating by text, on twitter, Facebook or any other form of social media.

- It is critical to the company that close attention is given to all public comments. The COO or Company Owners will handle all PR related issues. You must anticipate media coverage. Therefore, DO NOT accept phone calls from the media (newspapers, TV stations, radio stations, online sources, etc.).

- Employees should not, in any manner, interfere with the government's enforcement of the search warrant.

In order for us to effectively respond to the execution of a government search warrant, we will do the following:

- Educate personnel concerning search warrant preparedness in advance to:
- Call outside legal counsel immediately upon receiving the warrant;
- Identify the lead government investigator and all those involved with the warrant;
- Obtain a copy of the warrant and review it;
- Monitor the search as it is being executed and document everything that is seized. Note if seized items are privileged, confidential or critical to business operations; and
- Instruct employees to remain calm and cooperate with the government investigators executing the search and adhere to any advice given by counsel (that you should have already called).

Frequently Asked Questions (FAQs) About Regulatory Investigations

Some of the FAQs listed below suggest what to do when a regulator contacts the office. It is advisable to ask your supervisor, your company owner and/or your company Expert Attorney how to handle these situations. As additional questions arise, be sure to include them in your FAQs. Each company will customize their Policies and Procedures and FAQs  based on need and their owner's preferences and priorities.

What does a company employee do if a regulator calls?

First, remain calm. Transfer the call to the company Code Responsibility Officer/Administrator or Compliance Officer. If that contact is unknown, transfer the call to your immediate supervisor. Do not answer any questions or give names of department personnel except for the Compliance Department.
What does the Compliance Officer do if a regulator calls?

- First, remain calm. Gather as much information as the person is willing to share name, agency, department, phone, extension, email, and other information such as the reason for the call.
- If you are comfortable, answer basic level questions, if not, explain that you will need to have them talk to your supervisor.
- Ask them specifically what they need and make note.

What does the Compliance Officer do if a regulator comes to the office?

- First, remain calm! Instruct front desk staff to inform the company
- Compliance Officer that someone from (agency) is there to speak with them.
- If the regulators have a search warrant, remain calm and immediately notify your immediate supervisor and company owner, if on site.
- Ask permission of the regulatory person in charge for you to contact your MLM specialist attorney ASAP.
- Ask your company owner/supervisor if they want to talk to the company MLM specialist attorney and, if so, get them on the phone.

When does the Compliance Officer involve their supervisor and/or owner?

This notification occurs when the situation warrants such involvement and/or when the issue involves the media or any regulatory inquiry.

Chapter 9

LESSONS IN MISSING THE POINT
BY KEVIN GRIMES

*Why do MLM companies keep getting sued by the FTC for the same stuff
as others have been sued for decades?*

PART 1
The recent FTC v. Neora lawsuit raises a question - Do MLM leaders
(corporate executives and field leaders) "get it" when it comes to the
legal and regulatory requirements that govern MLMs?

In light of the long litigation history of the FTC against MLMs and
purported MLMs (JewelWay, FutureNet, Equinox, Fortune Hi-Tech
Marketing, BurnLounge, to name but a few), the answer seems to
historically be "No". In light of the recent litigation history against
several significant MLM companies (Vemma, Herbalife, AdvoCare,
and now Neora), the answer still seems to be "No".

When it comes to FTC enforcement actions, it appears to be different
day, different company, same stuff. The FTC is not bringing lawsuits
against MLM companies alleging completely new theories of law.
Yes, I concede that the FTC and the federal courts have been "moving

the goal line" with respect to what constitutes:

1. a pyramid; and
2. a legal MLM. However, one of the realities of the business world is that laws and legal standards evolve and change.

What is there about MLM legalities that MLM leaders do not know, do not want to know, or could not care less whether they know?

Having represented more than 1,000 MLM companies over the last 27 years, the intersection of MLM executives, entrepreneurs and field leaders, and MLM legalities is perhaps most appropriately called – *"Lessons in Missing the Point."*

For decades, the corporate and field leaders who manage and influence so many MLMs simply "don't get it" when it comes to MLM legalities. They think they do.

But the substantial factual regulatory fodder they provide to the FTC and federal courts says otherwise. If you ask the typical MLM exec or field leader exactly what the game- changing cases hold and what they mean for an MLM company's day-to-day operations, he or she cannot tell you.

The bottom line is -- Every federal case and FTC enforcement action is a seminal case!

If MLM leaders don't know what these cases say, how can they guide their companies and organizations toward compliance... and continued operation? What excuse is there for making the same mistakes over and over, year after year, decade after decade?

I am reminded of one of the greatest and simplest truths I have ever heard.

"Those who neglect history are doomed to repeat it."
-- GEORGE SANTAYANA

What is astounding to me is that many of the people who lead MLM companies are absolutely brilliant . . . but . . . epically poor students (or non-students) of MLM history. As such, they supply the unfortunate first ingredient of Mr. Santayana's quote. Consequently, we have seen the second part of Mr. Santayana's quote continue to unfold for the MLM industry during last three decades.

Being a poor student (or an unteachable student) of MLM history has the potential for a devastating effect. The purpose of this series of articles is to briefly review the history and messages of the last 23 years of FTC enforcement actions and federal court decisions, articulate the current state of the law (the vast majority of which continues to be ignored by most MLM companies), and propose appropriate   changes of operations to avoid FTC enforcement actions, class actions and other legal/regulatory problems.

The Lessons of History

This article will touch on a few of the important lessons and "takeaways" from MLM regulatory history. But it is too brief to address all of them. Accordingly, subsequent articles will address additional lessons, takeaways and strategies for decreasing regulatory and legal risks. (So, please come back next month.)

Lesson 1 - The Majority of Distributor Compensation MUST Be Derived from Sales to Customers (Non-Distributors).

As Nerium does in its very courageous and brilliant lawsuit against the FTC, we can debate whether this is the current federal legal standard for determining whether a program is legitimate MLM or a pyramid. What is not debatable is that the FTC is, and has been, suing MLM companies that fail to generate more than 50% of their revenues and more than 50% of all distributor compensation from sales to Customers.

The FTC's thinking is - If the majority (more than 50%) of distributor compensation does not flow from sales to customers, the program is not sales-based. If the program is not sales-based, it is de facto recruitment-based, and therefore, a pyramid.

We see this thinking reflected in paragraph 12 of the FTC's Complaint against Nerium. Purchases by BPs (Brand Partners) have accounted for more than half of all company revenues. In paragraph 123 of the Complaint, the FTC asserts that Nerium is a pyramid because participants "pay money to the company in return for which they receive . . . the right to receive rewards which are unrelated to the sale of products to the ultimate users."

The federal courts and the FTC have been banging the drum for pre-eminence of customer sales for 23 years! But the MLM industry has repeatedly turned a deaf ear to the increasingly shrill warnings of the federal courts and the FTC.

It started in 1996 in the infamous Webster v. Omnitrition decision, in which the U.S. Court of Appeals stated:

The key to any anti-pyramiding rule in a program like Omnitrition's, where the basic structure serves to reward recruitment more than retailing, is that the rule [compensation plan eligibility requirements] must serve to tie recruitment bonuses to actual retail sales in some way.

In the Omnitrition case we see the first indication from the federal courts regarding the "tying" of distributor compensation to sales to non-distributors - Customers. However, I will concede that the Court's language is about as imprecise as it can be – "tie recruitment bonuses to actual retail sales in some way."

What does "in some way" mean?
That question was answered elsewhere in the Omnitrition decision. Omnitrition (the company) argued that because it had the three

"Amway Rules" written into its contractual documents, as a matter of law, it could not be a pyramid. The Court of Appeals rejected that argument and wrote:

> ... *plaintiffs have produced evidence that the 70% rule can be satisfied by a distributor's personal use of the products. If Koscot is to have any teeth, such a sale [i.e., sales to distributors] cannot satisfy the requirement that sales be to "ultimate users" of a product.*

This called into question whether any personal product usage by distributors could be considered legitimate and legal.

What was the industry's response to the Omnitrition Court's admonition that compensation needed to be tied to retail sales? It completely ignored it.

Fast forward a few years to 2004. In the FTC's Staff Advisory Opinion - Pyramid Scheme Analysis to the Direct Selling Association, it wrote:

> *IN A PYRAMID SCHEME, participants hope to reap financial rewards well in excess of their investment based primarily on the fees paid by members of their "downlines". Downline members pay these fees to join the scheme and meet certain prerequisites for obtaining the monetary and other rewards offered by the program. A participant, therefore, can only reap rewards by obtaining a portion of the fees paid by those who join the scheme later. The people who join later, in turn, pay their fees in the hope of profiting from payments of those who enter the scheme after they do. In this way, a pyramid scheme simply transfers monies from losers to winners. For each person who substantially profits from the scheme, there must be many more losing all, or a portion, of their investment to fund those winnings. Absent sufficient sales of goods and services, the profits in such a system hinge on nothing more than recruitment of new participants (i.e., fee payers) into the system.*

The Commission's recent cases, however, demonstrate that the sale of goods and services alone does not necessarily render a multi-level system legitimate. Modem pyramid schemes generally do not blatantly base commissions on the outright payment of fees, but instead try to disguise those payments to appear as if they are based on the sale of goods or services. The most common means employed to achieve this goal is to require a certain level of monthly purchases to qualify for commissions. While the sale of goods and services nominally generates all commissions in a system primarily funded by such purchases, in fact, those commissions are funded by purchases made to obtain the right to participate in the scheme. Each individual who profits, there- fore, does so primarily from the payments of others who are themselves making payments in order to obtain their own profit. As discussed above, such a plan is little more than a transfer scheme, dooming the vast majority of participants to financial failure.

In the Staff Advisory Opinion, we see the FTC talking about "fees paid by members of their 'downlines'". In light of its claim that pyramids' try to disguise those payments to appear as if they are based on the sale of goods or services" and "the most common means employed to achieve this goal is to require a certain level of monthly purchases to qualify for commissions", it is clear that the FTC is saying that "fees paid by members'" can come from distributors' purchases of products. Moreover, the most significant factor that turns potentially legitimate personal purchases into recruitment-based fees are "certain level of monthly purchases to qualify for commissions".

Note also the FTC's comment, "Absent sufficient sales of goods and services, the profits in such a system hinge on nothing more than recruitment of new participants (i.e., fee payers) into the system."

Let's keep moving forward in time. What kind of language have we more recently seen coming from the federal courts and the FTC regarding the need for sales to, and compensation flowing from, customers?

FTC v. Vemma

On August 17, 2015, the FTC sued Vemma Nutrition Company and Vemma International Holdings (collectively "Vemma"). In its Complaint, the FTC alleged that Vemma was a pyramid and made false and misleading income claims. One month later, the U.S. District Court granted a preliminary injunction against Vemma. The Order mandated that the Defendants were:

. . . preliminarily restrained and enjoined from: A. Engaging in, participating in, or assisting others in engaging in or participating in, any Marketing Program that:

> *Pays any compensation related to the purchase or sale of goods or services unless the majority of such compensation is derived from sales to or purchases by persons who are not members of the Marketing Program; (Emphasis added.)*

In the Stipulated Order for Permanent Injunction, Vemma was permanently enjoined from paying... a participant any compensation related to the sale of goods or services in a fixed pay period unless the majority of the total revenue generated during such period by the participant and others within the participant's downline is derived from sales to persons who are not participants in the Business Venture.

The Bottom Line - In order for each individual distributor to be eligible to receive compensation, a U.S. District Court requires the majority of each distributor's compensation to come from sales to Customers.

FTC v. Herbalife

The Stipulation to Entry of Order for Permanent Injunction and Monetary Judgment (the "Herbalife Order") from the FTC v. Herbalife case limits the maximum amount of compensation an Herbalife Distributor can receive from her downline distributors' personal purchases to 1/3 of her entire downline volume. The Herbalife Order provides limitations on Multi-Level Compensation. The program shall include, and Defendants shall enforce, the following provisions:

Any Multi-Level Compensation paid to a Participant for a given period shall be generated solely by the following categories of transactions ("Rewardable Transactions") . . .

> *d. All or a portion of Rewardable Personal Consumption transactions, determined pursuant to Subsection I.E., of the Participant's Downline; provided that the Rewardable Personal Consumption transactions included in a Participant s Rewardable Transactions shall be limited such that no more than one-third of the total value of the Participant's Multi-Level Compensation may be attributable to or generated by such transactions.*

The Bottom Line - The FTC requires Herbalife to insure that at least two-thirds of a Distributor's compensable volume to come from sales to Customers.

The Take-Away

For 23 years, sales to customers, and most recently, having the majority of revenues derived from sales to customers, are essential to the legality of an MLM program. An MLM that does not have the majority of its sales revenues and distributor compensation derived from customer sales may be at risk for a regulatory challenge.

Lesson 2 - It is Not Only the Compensation Plan that Determines Whether an MLM is a Pyramid - How it Operates in Practice is.

Ultimate Determiner
As the U.S. Court of Appeals explained in the BurnLounge case,
To determine whether a MLM business is a pyramid, a court must look at how the MLM business operates in practice.

A proper analysis of the BurnLounge metrics is beyond the scope of this article, but will be discussed in a future article. In summary, the BurnLounge Metrics are:

- The value of the company's products
- The operational realities
- Who is buying what and how much?
- The products or services cannot be a sham or smoke screen for a "pay-to-play" scheme
- Some sales to non-distributors (customers) are not enough
- Required purchases for distributors
- Comp plan rules to promote retail sales
- Meaningful opportunities for retail sales

In addition to the BurnLounge metrics, some additional "operational realities" about which the FTC has complained or a court has found problematic include:

- Overemphasis on distributor recruiting
- Inadequate emphasis on customer acquisition and customer sales
- Large product pack purchases by distributors (not in the thousands of dollars, but in the hundreds)
- Allowing distributors to "buy their way" to higher ranks in the compensation plan
- Overemphasis on distributor auto-ship participation
- Awarding a lower amount of PV or BV on Customer purchases versus Distributor purchases
- High personal volume requirements and a failure to track sales to end consumers
- Failure to enforce anti-inventory loading safeguards, such as the 70% Rule and 10 Customer Rule
- Inadequate refund and buy-back policies
- Lack of regulatory compliance training for distributors

It is worth noting that there are other operational realities the FTC has highlighted in its complaints to buttress patterns of deception and violation of the FTC Act, including deceptive income claims (perennial low-hanging fruit for the FTC) and lack of adequate substantiation for product claims.

Conclusion

In future articles, we will look at issues related to income claims, auto-ship orders, substantiation for product claims, product packs, fast start bonuses and a long list of other operational realities that are providing ample ammunition to regulators and class action attorneys.

As I mentioned at the beginning of this article, one of the realities of the business world is that laws and legal standards evolve and change. Although the legal and regulatory requirements for MLM programs have changed substantially over the 23 year, for the MLM industry, it continues to be "business as usual".

It is long past the time when MLM companies should have re-set their sails and adjusted their paradigms and business practices. George Santayana was right - Those who neglect history are doomed repeat it. As we have seen from recent FTC cases, the consequences can be extreme.

- Trek Alliance - out of business
- BurnLounge - out of business
- Vemma - out of business
- Herbalife - $200 million for equitable monetary relief, sweeping changes to its compensation plan, an FTC mandated compliance training program
- Advocare - $150 million for equitable monetary relief and completely out of MLM
- Nerium – as of this writing still in the courts.

Dinosaurs could not adapt to climate change and they are now extinct. MLM companies that fail to adjust to the current climate change may also become extinct.

MLM companies must take an absolutely comprehensive and holistic approach to regulatory compliance. At the risk of sounding completely self-serving, all corporate resources (not merely the compensation plan) need to be reviewed for legal compliance. This means all videos, the entire website, all promotional materials, and all training resources should be reviewed by MLM counsel. Companies must be equally vigilant with respect to distributor compliance - training, monitoring, correcting and sanctioning (where appropriate) distributor activities.

The proverbial handwriting is on the wall.
In the fifth chapter of the Book of Daniel in the Old Testament, Belshazzar, the King of Babylon witnessed the supernatural handwriting on the wall of his palace. The inscription said:

Mene, Mene, Tekel, Parsin

Neither Belshazzar nor his advisors could interpret the message. So they called for Daniel who explained the meaning of the words.

Mene: God has numbered the days of your reign and brought it to an end.
Tekel: You have been weighed on the scales and found wanting.
Parsin: Your kingdom is divided and given to the Medes and Persians.

Belshazzarís unwillingness to humble himself and change was ultimately the cause of his downfall.
May it not be so for MLM.

Let's do it right!

Kevin D. Grimes - Thompson Burton, PLLC

Chapter 10

SHOULDA ... WOULDA!

THESE ACCOUNTS ARE BASED on true experiences. The names and locations have been changed to protect some of the mentioned parties. Some have been identified due to being out of business for years.

The Invisible Product:

In 1999 SOHO (Small Office Home Office) company P.R.S.I. sold computer-generated websites to over 48,000 people at $295.00 each, (NOT Customers) they were ALL Distributors; collecting over $13 million in their first year. They paid out commission without providing the product. The product NEVER existed and was NEVER delivered. They were selling air.

Outcome: On January 2, 2000, the Florida Attorney General raided their offices in Fort Lauderdale and shut them down. The Florida Authorities kicked in the doors with MP-5's (machine guns) in their hands. I can testify to this since I was there. I was hired in November of 1999 to assist Garry Nehra in developing the company's legal document; but it was just too little too late.

The authorities took the computers, the cell phones and the phone system into their control. They seized all the money that was left, and froze all the assets of the owner and the upper management (including their wives accounts). The owner was convicted of securities fraud and went to prison for over 10 years. The CFO, who was a relative, implicated himself in the scam. The company's upper management did not protect their assets. Since all their money was seized, and they had no funds left for their legal defense they were all in vulnerable positions.

The Invisible Investment

This company was in the start-up phase and needed operating capital. They defrauded 20 people out of $15,000 each, making all of them Master Distributors. They promised the participants huge downline organizations. All they had to do was pay the $15,000 and the company would be an ATM of never-ending money. The money disappeared. The company never got off the ground.

Outcome: It was no surprise that the owners were known to the authorities. They fled, and no money was recovered.

The Invisible Policy

This growing company had 1,000 Distributors. One of the leading Distributors had a compliance violation. The owner terminated a Distributor by having a non-MLM Expert Attorney write a three-page termination letter.

The Distributors exposed the owner's termination letter on social media. This caused an uproar within the company's Distributor base. The owner had no direct selling compliance experience or documentation, she had nothing to build her case on or justify the termination.

Outcome: The company lost almost half of the Distributorship force within two months. Having to rectify this complicated situation, the growth of the company was dramatically delayed and within 6 months the company shut its door down as a Direct Selling Company.

The Invisible PR Department

This promising company had 6,000 Distributors worldwide (NOT customers) paying $100 a month in recurring product charges. The owner mishandled an overseas compliance issue and would not pay a distributor money he was owed. The procedure to solve the problem was not followed. A Distributor tried to blackmail the owner to get his money. When his plan didn't work, the Distributor notified the authorities and the media to initiate an investigation of the company as a pyramid scheme.

Outcome: The company lost 1,000 Distributors within 30-days and the company closed shortly after that, due to the negative publicity and looming compliance issues. They also were playing close to some legal lines and decided to shut down before they were closed by legal action.

The Invisible Brain

This company, American Petroleum Products (APP), was doing well with expert legal advice. The owner single-handedly changed the compensation plan. He was then advised by the expert attorney that his actions were not defendable. The attorney withdrew counsel. The owner proceeded with his plan.

Outcome: The regulators initiated an in-depth investigation. The Owner was caught without any defense for his actions. It was no surprise that the booming company went out of business.

The Invisible Budget

This company was under-financed from the beginning and the owner thought that micro-managing the Distributors would allow her to run the company on a shoestring. The product sold itself, the financing was not secure, and the distributors were doing whatever they wanted to make sales. The owner took out a second mortgage on her own home and lost all of the money.

Outcome: The owner shut down the company and sold off the inventory for pennies on the dollar.

The Invisible Customer Service

This company had 3,000 Distributors who were uneducated as to the proper, legal marketing techniques. They provided poor customer service; treated the customers and Distributors as if they were annoying and unnecessary. Distributors were allowed to make medical claims, unauthorized social media posts and run opportunity meetings without compliance direction.

Outcome: The Distributors rebelled against the company and complained to regulators about poor billing procedures and unavailable customer service. The company survived with minimal growth and with no compliance direction.

In Summary

Some of the biggest names in the Direct Selling (MLM) industry already have landed in the crosshairs of FTC compliance scrutiny. Size or scale does not matter. Why? Because some executives thought the laws did not apply to them, or it was no big deal, or perhaps just didn't know. As the industry experiences a global explosion and the anticipated growth is projected to reach $1Trillion (USD), FTC and lawmakers have sharpened their focus to ensure illegal management and system policies do not taint an otherwise viable and lucrative industry. Unlike other industries, where everything is about the products and the *"You create it and they will come"* attitude prevails, a direct selling company must establish clear and comprehensive compliance structures, and all the elements that it impacts.

As we have noted throughout this book, the legal responsibilities and implications are high. Everyone across the organization, from the founder, to marketers and distributors must not only understand legal compliance but they are bound by its limitations or restrictions – there are no exceptions. The #1 area that can make or break your company is *Compliance* and it has already brought down some of the biggest, multi-million dollar companies. Make sure you get the support and guidance required to develop and maintain a compliance plan for your company's success. We are here for you!

COMPLIANCE MANAGEMENT SYSTEM

Our Contributors

Gerry Nehra
Law Offices of Nehra and Waak
gnehra@mlmatty.com | www.mlmatty.com
231-755-3800

Mr. Nehra is an MLM Expert Attorney in private practice in Muskegon, Michigan and Sarasota, Florida. He is one of a few attorneys nationwide whose practice is devoted exclusively to direct selling and multi-level marketing matters. His 46 years of legal experience includes 9-years at Amway Corporation where he was Director of the Legal Division.

Gerry and I met years ago on one of my very first cases. He has, over the years, taught me volumes in the direct selling industry. Gerry was the first call I made when I was at the wrong place at the wrong time. I was in Fort Lauderdale, FL, it was January 2000 and one of our mutual clients was raided by regulators. What an experience that was being on the inside looking out. With Gerry pointing me in the right direction, I was able to work directly with the attorneys on the case after the shutdown. It was a world of education on MLM Compliance and believe it not, it was a most interesting look at our regulatory process.

Kevin Thompson: Thompson –Burton, PLLC
MLM Expert Attorney
kthompson@thompsonburton.com
(615) 465-6000
| https://thompsonburton.com

Kevin Thompson is an MLM attorney, proud husband, father of three, and a founding member of Thompson Burton PLLC and named as one of the top 25 most influential people in direct sales. Kevin Thompson has extensive experience to help entrepreneurs launch their businesses on secure legal footing. Recently featured on CNBC with Herb Greenberg, Thompson is a thought-leader in the industry.

In a prior life, Kevin was an accomplished track athlete at the University of Tennessee, garnering All-American honors in the Decathlon. Kevin developed his passion for direct sales as an Amway Distributor, selling energy drinks and doing anything possible to earn extra cash while in school. With his competitive nature, Kevin was drawn to the world of working with young network marketing companies trying to make a difference selling superior products and services through networks of people. As a DSA supplier member, Kevin Thompson is actively involved on the Ethics Committee and Government Relation Board to help steer the industry into a promising future. He has served as a keynote speaker for clients all across the world.

Prior to starting his law practice, Kevin gained valuable experience while serving as Chief Counsel for Signature Management Team, LLC, also known as Team. Team is one of the largest providers of sales aids for Distributors in the network marketing industry. While at Team, Kevin worked closely with Amway and Mona Vie's Compliance Departments to ensure Team's marketing materials passed regulatory review. Also, during his tenure at Team, Kevin helped guide the company through commercial litigation with Amway. He has the experience, knowledge, connections and tools necessary to help entrepreneurs securely launch their businesses.

And if none of that is enough. Kevin serves on the Young Executive Leadership Team for Youth Villages in Nashville, Tennessee where he helps devise and execute programs to raise funds for the organization that create transitional living programs for abandoned and neglected teens.

Kevin Grimes: MLM Expert Attorney
Redefining the Art of Law
Phone - (615) 465-6000 x 208
Direct Dial - (208) 524-1008
Email: kgrimes@thompsonburton.com
Web: www.thompsonburton.com

Kevin Grimes is one of the most experienced and accomplished MLM attorneys in America. Over his 23-year career as a network marketing attorney, he has represented and advised the proverbial "Who's Who" of direct selling and multilevel marketing including Herbalife, Shaklee, Tupperware, USANA, MetaboLife, Mona Vie, and hundreds more.

He's a frequent contributor to the industry, serving as the co-author of the definitive direct selling legal Website MLMLaw.com, and numerous MLM legal resources including; MLMComplianceVT.com, "Legal Do's and Don'ts for Network Marketers" and "What to Look for and What to Look Out for in Multilevel Marketing."

In addition to specializing in direct selling and network marketing law, he services several areas frequently associated with them including: consumer protection for food, drug, cosmetic, and dietary supplement law as well as distributor compliance. Perhaps the single-most uniquely important aspect of the talents and experience Kevin brings to the table is that, prior to joining the industry as an attorney, he was a distributor for two large direct selling organizations, Amway and Nikken, building his last organization up to a group volume of over $40,000 per month.

Prior to joining Thompson Burton, Kevin was a member of Grimes & Reese. He has served as Assistant General Counsel for Melaleuca since 1992, advising senior sales management on sales and marketing issues, regulatory matters, distributor compliance, and international law. In the early 80s Kevin served as an U.S. Army Staff Judge Advocate General's Corp, where he successfully managed and defended a claims portfolio exceeding $50 million, resulting in the payment of no settlements or judgments.

His Area of Expertise:
- Compensation Plans
- Distributor Compliance
- Advertising Law
- Regulatory Investigations
- International Expansion
- Contests/Sweepstakes
- Distributor Training
- Vendor Contract FDA/FTC law

Kevin is a graduate of Southern Methodist University School of Law ('85), and Colorado College ('82). Kevin has been a member of the Direct Selling Association – Lawyers' Council and Government Relations Committee.

Aside from being a great lawyer, Kevin has a passion for helping abandoned teens. He's been serving as a foster parent for 13-years and has fostered 24 teenage boys (and bears several scars to prove it).

Scott Burnett: Asset Protection Attorney
Scott@BurnettandAssociates.com
775-853-6999

Recognized as "one of the nation's leading asset protection attorneys", Scott is a lawyer with almost 25-years of civil and criminal litigation experience. Early in his career Mr. Burnett was a Deputy District Attorney in Santa Barbara, California with a perfect trial record. In his private practice as a personal injury attorney, his law firm collected several millions of dollars in settlements and judgments. He now teaches business owners how to protect their assets from litigation and frivolous lawsuits.

Scott is considered to be one of the leading authorities on asset protection and tax education for corporation and LLC's in the country. He currently sits on the Board of Directors for over 200 separate businesses. His ability to explain complicated material in an uncomplicated and entertaining manner has made him a highly sought after trainer and speaker throughout the country.

RESOURCES

www.DirectSellingSolutions.com

Direct Selling Solutions Services

Direct Selling Solutions and its network of industry experts is the premier company to assist your direct selling company with any compliance need. From start-up, to implementation and ongoing management we possess the experience, expertise and reputation, to ensure your company has a successful Compliance Department and never faces an FTC inquiry. Direct Selling Solutions offers Direct Selling Companies three levels of service:

1. Compliance Start-Up Solutions: Design and launch your Compliance Department
    a. Formation of the Compliance Action Plan
    b. Development of the "Policies at a Glance"
    c. Set up monitoring SOPs for Social Media
    d. Review of legal documentation
2. Compliance Management Solutions: On going Management Oversight and Updates
    a. Ongoing Compliance Department education and support
    b. Compliance Department Coordinators & Analysts
    c. The Compliance Management System (CMS)
    d. Monthly Compliance Corner Education
3. Ultimate Compliance Solutions: The *Complete* Compliance Package
    a. The Compliance Audit- Full Legal Review for larger companies

b. Assistance for emergent regulatory issues
c. Includes all the Start Up Solutions and the Management Solutions

Direct Selling Solutions offers a full range of services *ESPECIALLY* to manage Independent Distributors such as:

1. Compliance Checkups
2. Social Media Sweeps
3. What to Say – What Not to Say Training
4. Detailed Compliance Reporting
5. Field Leadership Training
6. Termination Review
7. Compliance Video Reviewing

 **The Direct Selling Edge Conference**
www.directsellingedge.com

Exceptional education for Start-Up Direct Selling Companies Become wiser by attending the Direct Selling Edge Conference held for owners and employees of new and established direct selling companies. Presented by Sylvina Consulting and Thompson Burton since 2011

What people say about the Direct Selling Edge

"What a great group of speakers! Jay Leisner is a great teacher and has a strong, experienced perspective on Direct Sales. I learned a lot from Kevin Grimes and Jeff Jordan that I needed to learn. Scott Burnett and Troy Dooly were very inspiring and personable. Donna Marie Serritella was a perfect

afternoon speaker to keep us engaged and interested. I also enjoyed the experience to be able to ask everyone questions afterwards. Thank you!"

Denise

"I was amazed at the information. I thought it was going to be a broad stroke event to get you with different vendors. I was very surprised to see all of the targeted topics, how in-depth they went into discussing very important issues, for anyone who is considering getting into the MLM business as a startup company. It's one of the best conferences that I have ever been to."

Mike

 **The Direct Selling Edge Faculty**

Jay Leisner
jay@sylvina.com | 503.244.8787
Sylvina Consulting | www.sylvina.com

Jay Leisner, the president of Sylvina Consulting, is a top compensation plan and direct selling expert, a trusted adviser to new and established network marketing and party plan companies. For more than 30 years, Jay has enjoyed assessing and improving party plan and network marketing companies across the globe.

Compensation plan design and evaluation, business plan development and forecasting, improvement of marketing and training materials, direct selling coaching, software evaluation and selection, and business performance evaluations are most frequently requested services.

Sylvina Consulting also publishes the top-rated 250-page direct selling startup book, Start Here: The Guide For Building and Growing Your Direct Selling Company. Previous to launching Sylvina Consulting, Jay worked for 13 years with a major direct selling software provider as a software developer, project leader and business analyst to provide both startups and existing companies, in the USA and abroad, with customized software solutions to meet the requirements of their businesses.

Along the way while working with them, he learned the secrets of successful direct selling companies and the challenges faced by them. In true entrepreneurial spirit, Jay's decision in 1999 to start Sylvina Consulting as a direct selling consulting company was driven by what he saw was a need for answers, advice, and solutions.

More than just a compensation plan expert, Jay is exceptionally skilled at advising new and established companies on business strategies. Before offering advice or solutions, he asks important questions to understand each client's specific concerns and goals.

Troy Dooly: Beachside CEO
Troy@BeachsideCEO.com | 850.462.EPIC
(3742) www.beachsideceo.com
Eight Pillars of Iconic Companies

Named One of the most influential voices in the world by critics and proponents alike, Troy Dooly is Co-Founder and the Beachside CEO of the global advisory agency, Lighthouse Idea Crafters, an organization whose sole focus is to help guide organizations to develop cultures which enhance customer experience and increase shareholder value.

Troy has emerged as a leading authority in the area of development of purpose-inspired cultures. Startup entrepreneurs to multinational corporations have adopted his breakthrough methodology and frameworks to protect their teams' integrity and to deliver real difference to the people serve. Troy's creed is "Living an Epic Adventure" - in work or life; follow your passion, and live your purpose.

When Troy isn't working with clients, he is a speaker, results coach, radio and TV host. He was a founding show host and News Director of the Home Business Radio Network. A founding member, of the Association of Network Marketing Professionals, a Direct Sales Hall of Fame inductee, faculty member of the DS Edge educational organization, and ranked in the top 2500 influencers across the world wide web.

Troy is also founding member of Catalyst A-Team, helping to facilitate hundreds of volunteers annually who serve 10,000 to 13,000 guests at the Atlanta Catalyst Leadership Conference. Troy has been married 31 years, to his high school sweetheart, and bestselling author, Paige Winship Dooly. They have eight wonderful children, and a dozen grandchildren.

Jerry York: ByDesign Technologies
jerry@bydesign.com | 813.253.2235:
www.bydesign.com
Nine Things You Must Know Before
Buying MLM Software

Jerry York is the Vice President of Sales at ByDesign Technologies. His career in Network Marketing and Party Plan spans over 35-years with extensive experience in the field as a distributor, the owner of his own network marketing company, and as an executive with three software information systems providers.

Jerry has worked closely with start-up companies as well as large, established, international DSA companies. He has published several articles on the industry, and has spoken worldwide on building strong and lasting downlines. Jerry has been an integral part of the ByDesign team since 2004.

Jeff Jordan

jeffs56@me.com | 480.225.4065
Jordan & Associates |
www.jeffjordanmlmconsultant.com

Jeff Jordan is a 25-years plus veteran of the direct sales/network marketing Industry. He started as an independent distributor and within a few short months had achieved top ranks and qualified for the company's automobile program. After a successful run as a top distributor, Jeff joined a network marketing training company as VP of Sales and later became Executive VP. Jeff later left the training company to again build a network marketing organization where he and his wife had the fastest growing organization in the company, where was appointed National Director of Training. Jeff went on to become a direct selling consultant specializing in sales, training, and top distributor recruitment programs. Jeff has also served on more than one occasion as founder and executive of direct selling companies.

Today, Jeff Jordan focuses on his consulting practice, focused as an Interim Vice President of Sales for a few different direct selling companies, which affords his clients the VP of Sales & Marketing expertise without the expense of hiring a full time executive.

Emily Barr: Orbis Consulting Services
emily@orbisconsultingservices.com
443.865.5885
http://www.orbisconsultingservices.com
Direct Selling Operations: On Time and On Budget

Emily Barr is an operational efficiency specialist with 10 years of direct selling experience. She successfully led the operational launch of two direct selling startups. Emily also has experience creating operational improvements and efficiencies for Fortune 500 companies. Her operational and strategic sales experience allows her to very quickly identify solutions to problems. She has the innate ability to identify trends, create sales strategy recommendations based on data and analysis, and execute on those strategic plans.

Emily enjoys sharing her knowledge in the areas of inventory management, support systems, compensation plans, recognition, incentives, and process documentation for startups and established companies looking to create efficiencies.

Daryl Wurzbacher, CEO: ByDesign Technologies
daryl@bydesign | 813.253.2235
www.ByDesign.com

Daryl began his direct selling career on the client side of the industry in 1999 as the Director of IT for a new company whose sales grew to $70 million. In 2007, Daryl joined ByDesign as its Director of Technology. His strong work ethic and passion for continuous self-development led to increasing levels of responsibility and promotions to Vice-President of Applications and Platforms. Strategic leadership, innovation and energetic contributions let to his appointment as President and CEO in 2018.

Former Faculty Members

Karen Clark: My Business Presence
karen@mybusinesspresence.com 707.588.9290
www.mybusinesspresence.com Social Media Best Practices

Karen Clark is the founder of My Business Presence, a Social Media training company. She began her direct selling career as an independent representative who in just seven years achieved the highest rank in her company's compensation plan. After that, Karen held a position with the same party plan  company as the Director of Consultant Development for five years responsible for creating training programs for the field.

Now a sought-after speaker and distributor trainer, Karen works with the independent consultants of direct selling companies to master the world of internet marketing, including the effective use of Social Media. Karen has co-authored two books: Incredible Business and Direct Selling Power.

Karen's wealth of practical knowledge and ability to simplify even the most advanced Social Media concepts along with her fun friendly training style, will inspire you and your independent representatives to build relationships using smart Social Media strategies.

ABOUT THE AUTHOR
"THE QUEEN OF COMPLIANCE"
Donna Marie Serritella

Since 1991, Donna Marie Serritella of Direct Selling Solutions has assisted direct selling companies and leading Distributors in the areas of compliance consulting, distributor compliance relations, specializing in the training of Distributors and staff. She has authored a Compliance Management Manual that will refine all compliance efforts of the direct selling industry.

Donna Marie is a proud Board Member of the SNA: Social Networking Association. The Social Networking Association is a community of social influencers, companies, and support companies who have joined forces to positively impact the direct sales/network marketing/party plan industry. SNA was initially founded in 1985 as the MLMIA, Doris Wood and the board sought to meet the emotional, social, educational, and business needs of its members. At its height, the MLMIA had 87 social networking companies, 118 support companies, and many distributors.

The 35-year-old organization is being relaunched and rebranded as the Social Networking Association. Distributors, support, and Corporate entities voted and secured representation, making the association a formidable, united force in business. For more information, please visit www.snamembers.com

As a compliance expert, Donna Marie works with companies and legal advisors to either structure or improve their company operations to ensure the direct selling industry's legal compliance guidelines. Donna Marie was a contributing author of two chapters in the book, "Build it Big 101 Insider Secrets from Top Direct Selling Experts".

Donna Marie currently handles compliance for several direct selling companies. She also teaches individuals how to select the right direct selling company for them, as well as about the many benefits of being in a home-based business.

Connect with Donna Marie Serritella
DirectSellingSolutions@gmail.com
24/7 Access: http://www.directsellingsolutions.com/

facebook.com/DirectSellingSolutions
twitter.com/DMSerritella
instagram.com/DonnaMarieSolutions

NOTES

Direct Selling in a Social Media World
1. Ali, F., (2019). U.S. E-Commerce Sales Grow 15.0% in 2018, https://www.digitalcommerce360.com/article/us-ecommerce-sales/

11. Lessons in Missing the Point
There are unquestionably flaws in the FTC's logic, but time and space do not permit me to address those flaws herein. Admittedly, there is a massive error in the FTC's logic. In the BurnLounge case, the FTC argued that "internal sales to other Moguls [distributors] cannot be sales to ultimate users consistent with Koscot." The U.S. Court of Appeals rejected the FTC's position, saying that it was not supported by case law. The Court stated that, "[w]hether the rewards are related to the sale of products depends on how BurnLounge's bonus structure operated in practice. "Nevertheless, it seems clear that the FTC is unwilling to acknowledge that some distributors can be "ultimate users" under the right circumstances.

Eight years after the Omnitrition decision, the FTC issued an Advisory Memorandum to the Direct Selling Association regarding (in part) the issue of distributor personal consumption. The FTC wrote:

> *Much has been made of the personal, or internal, consumption issue in recent years. In fact, the amount of internal consumption in any multi-level compensation business does not determine whether or not the FTC will consider the plan a pyramid scheme. The critical question for the FTC is whether the revenues that primarily support the commissions paid to all participants are generated from purchases of goods and services that are not simply incidental to the purchase of the right to participate in a money-making venture.*

Evidently, the FTC was not satisfied that the one-third/two-thirds provision by itself was sufficient to stop all of the problematic aspects of the Herbalife business model. The Herbalife Order also: (1) flushed any non-Rewardable Personal Consumption volume in excess of 1/3 of total organization volume; (2) prohibited Herbalife distributors from participating in an autoship program; (3) capped the maximum volume from a Distributor's personal purchases that would be compensated via the compensation plan to $200 during the Herbalife Order's first 12 months, and a lower threshold thereafter; (4) mandated that points [i.e., PV, BV, etc.] from distributor purchases and customer purchase be equal; (5) prohibited the automatic transition from a Distributor to a Preferred Customer, or from a Preferred Customer to a Distributor; (6) mandated the collection and verification of sales transaction data for Preferred Customers and retail customers; (7) allowed compensation plan eligibility criteria to be satisfied only by sales to Preferred Customers [that is to say, volume generated by Distributors does not count toward compensation plan volume requirements].

FTC v. BurnLounge, 753 F.3d 878 (9th Cir. 2014); Webster v. Omnitrition International, 79 F.3d 776, 783-84 (9th Cir. 1996); see also United States v. Gold Unlimited, Inc., 177 F.3d 472, 479-82 (6th Cir. 1999); In re Amway Corp., 93 F.T.C. 618, 716 (1979).

Made in the USA
Monee, IL
14 August 2020